SALTWATER
FISHING
A TACTICAL APPROACH

SALTWATER FISHING
A TACTICAL APPROACH

A GUIDE FOR BEACH AND BOAT FISHERMEN

CAPTAIN JIM FREDA, CAPTAIN GENE QUIGLEY,
SHELL E. CARIS

BURFORD BOOKS

Printed in the United States of America.

10   9   8   7   6   5   4   3   2   1

Library of Congress Cataloging-in-Publication Data
Freda, Jim.
    Saltwater fishing : a tactical approach / Jim Freda,
  Gene Quigley, and Shell E. Caris.
        p.   cm.
    ISBN 1-58080-126-9 (pbk.)
    1. Saltwater fishing.   I. Quigley, Gene.   II. Caris, Shell E.
  III. Title.

  SH457.F74   2004
  799.16—dc22

                                    2004012949

Contents

Part V: The Guide's Approach—Techniques and Strategies

This book would not have come about without some very special people in our lives who have influenced us, helped us, or shared with us their knowledge and expertise in this sport. Many gave of their time or showed a genuine concern for our love of saltwater fishing and went the extra mile for us to help make us successful. We are indebted to all these special people, both from the professional arena and in our personal lives. We would like to extend our sincere gratitude to them.

PROFESSIONAL

We would like to acknowledge Bob Popovics for his never-ending support, friendship, and knowledge of saltwater fly fishing. To our minds, there is no better ambassador of the sport. He has taught us all so much about saltwater fly fishing. We truly treasure your friendship and guidance.

To our friends at Schrader Yacht Sales: Al Frandano, Ray Schrader, Karyn Carney, Pat Barry, Ed Pfleger, Kevin Schrader, Tony Schwertheim, and Carl Koch. We could not operate our business without you. Thank you for always keeping our boats in perfect working order.

To Linwood Parker, Robin Parker, and Jeff Pilcher of Parker Boats, we greatly appreciate all your support. Thanks you for building such tremendous boats.

To Rich Belanger and Dave Colley of the St. Croix Rod Company, thank you for all your support over the years, and for giving us and the industry such quality fishing rods.

To Bill Dawson of WD Dawsons for your ongoing, never-ending support and friendship.

To John Harder and Simon Gawesworth of Rio Fly Lines for your assistance with our fly school and guide service.

To George Valentini of G & B Fishing Systems and AVET Reels for your continual support and for all of our inshore and offshore AVET conventional reels.

To Joshua Scheinbaum of Aussie Tackle and Spotters Sunglasses for equipping us with the finest sunglasses on the market today. As guides, our eyes are among our most important tools, and you have them covered.

To Brian Chaney of Korkers footwear, thank you for keeping us safe on the rocks with Korkers.

To Gary Heger and his staff at Catalogue Publishers, thank you for your friendship and for keeping our name out there in your brochures.

To our good friend Bob D'Amico of Stripersurf.com, thank you for all the exposure you have given us on one of the finest striped bass Web sites in the nation: www.stripersurf.com.

To the Tibor Reel Company for your continual support.

To Tress Lutgen of Stowaway2.com, thank you for providing your cargo carrier for our gear.

To Scott Leon and Jessica Chapman of *Fly Fishing in Saltwaters* magazine, John Randolph, Ross Purnell, and Jay Nichols of *Fly Fisherman* magazine, Pete Barrett and Jim Hutchinson, Jr., of *The Fisherman* magazine, Bill Donovan of *New Jersey Angler* magazine, Nick Pullano of *New Jersey Boating and Fishing* magazine, Karen Jett of *Delaware Bay Angler* magazine, Karen Wall of the *Asbury Park Press*, Mitch Krugel and John Balkun of the *Bergen Record*, and Jim Manser of the *Coast Star* newspaper, thank you for allowing us to write for you.

To Bob Korlishen of the Gazillion Group, Hoboken, New Jersey, for designing a cover that we feel captures the character of fishing the Northeast Coast.

To the Professional Fly and Light Tackle Guides Association and all of its members for continually representing fly- and light-tackle-fishing guides with integrity, character, and professionalism.

And to our publisher Peter Burford, thank you for having the confidence in us to do this work.

PERSONAL

Captain Gene Quigley

To my lovely wife, Cecilia, and my sons and future fishing partners, Patrick and Justin. Thank you for your patience and support with my passion for fishing. I love you all dearly.

To my father and best friend, Gene Quigley Sr., thank you for teaching me to always follow my passion in life and for always being there for me. You are my hero.

To my mother, Elizabeth Quigley, thank you for introducing me to and sharing your love for the ocean with me. I love you dearly. To my sisters Melissa and Tana, all of your love and support will always be cherished.

To my uncle Michael Ferro Jr., for showing me the wonderful world of offshore fishing, and for taking me fishing with you when I was a young boy.

To my great-uncle the late Phil Panzera, for holding the rod when I was too little to do it by myself.

To my grandfather Michael Ferro Sr., for passing on your passion for the sea to me, and for your never-ending love and support.

To the late Bill Pardini for teaching me all about the ocean, and for introducing me to surf fishing.

To Harry Huff for releasing the fly-fishing animal in me during the early years. Thank you for giving me my first fly rod and for teaching me to cast and tie flies.

To all my fishing buddies: Bob Popovics, Tom McGinley, Lance Irwin, Dino Torino, Dave Kusel, Pete Destefano, Dave Goldman, Jim and Alice Ardito, Tim Byrne, Al Frandano, John Szot, Bill Hoblitzell, Dean Nelson, Peter McCarthy, John Yavorsky, Darin Muly, Terry Kiley, Jim Spollen, and others. Thanks for all the good times and great fishing memories.

And to my partners at Shore Catch, Capt. Jim Freda and Shell E. Caris, thank you for your great friendship and fishing memories.

Shell E. Caris

To my parents, and especially my late father, Bernie Caris, who introduced me to striped bass fishing at the age of seven. From that day on I was hooked for life. Next I would like to thank my loving wife, Bonnie, for her support and encouragement day in and day out for more than 36 years. Also, my wonderful children, Adam and Jennifer, whom I admire deeply.

Special thanks to Brian R. Schneider for his help with the ideas and layout of some of this book, and the illustrations: "I couldn't have done it without him." My good friends and partners Gene Quigley and Jimmy Freda. And to all my fishing buddies who over the years helped make this book a reality.

Captain Jim Freda

First and foremost I would like to praise and thank God for being the sovereign God that He is. I thank Him for His love in sending His Son, our Lord and Savior Jesus Christ, to die for our sins so that we might be saved.

To my wife, Mary, and my children, Christie, Carlie, and Thomas James. Thank you for your love, support, and allowing me to fish. I love you dearly and look forward to many fishing memories together.

To my dad, Babe Freda, for his many trips taking me to Verona Park when I first started to fish, and my mom, Anne Freda, for always packing me a lunch to take along. Thank you both for your love and support. Those memories will last forever, as will my love for you. To my brother, Carmine Freda, who always accompanied me on those trips as we caught fish together. I was never alone. And to my sisters, Debbie Gallo, Patty Pietrobon, Anne Marie Freda, and Edna Cullen, thank you for the wonderful memories growing up together.

To Pastor Randy Smith and all my brothers and sisters at Grace Tabernacle, thank you for holding me accountable to the Word.

To my partners Gene and Shell E., you have been great friends and fishing buddies.

To our good friend and fellow Shore Catch captain David Goldman: It's been great growing up and fishing and now working together.

To our friends and fellow Shore Catch guides, Darin Muly, and Drew Ciok, thank you for your dedication to Shore Catch and help in making it what it is today.

To my fishing buddies Augie Scafidi, John Fields, John Scharff, Kevin Hyland, Captain Frank Bovasso, Randy Smith, Joe Kane, Tommy Grasso, Chuck Furimsky, Adam Pharo, Bobby Matthews, and especially Tom Paglioroli who started me fishing back in grammar school, the late Rocky Luciano who shared so much of his fishing knowledge with me, and Tom Westervelt for the many hours spent fishing together outside with the Lord.

Fishing is one of the largest recreational sports in the country; it can boast of millions of people partaking in it every year. Each season the numbers of participants grow and the industry reaches new levels. For some, the excitement, relaxation, and camaraderie that the sport has to offer cannot be matched by any other pastime or endeavor.

Many have poured their hearts and souls into this sport, calling it an obsession, while others have made it a profession. But although the experience may be different for each of us, we all are working toward the same end: catching fish.

One of the beauties of this sport is that there are many different methods available. There is no "one way" or set of specific rules you must follow to be successful on the water. There are, however, some time-proven tips and tactics that will outproduce all other methods at specific times and locations.

Many of these tips and tactics are learned by anglers only after long hours of trial and error and as a result have become well-guarded secrets. Still, some fishers are more than willing to share their experiences to shorten the learning curve for others. As a result, revealing guarded secrets or locations has always been a point of contention among anglers.

We here at Shore Catch entered into this sport with the fisherman in mind. Simply put, we want to share our love for and dedication to this sport with all those who come into contact with us. The best way for us to do this is to share all the knowledge we have acquired over the years with you. We believe that by cooperatively working together, all of us will catch more fish.

For this reason, we bring to you *Saltwater Fishing: A Tactical Approach*. This is not an A–Z encyclopedia that teaches you the basics of this sport; rather, it is a book that reveals many time-proven advanced tactics that have worked for us in the Northeast.

Our book works off the premise that you have some prior fishing-related experience and have put in your time on the water while catching your share of fish. Yet you're looking to take your fishing experience to the next level. Whether it's how to catch more fish, correcting bad habits, or just learning more of what this sport has to offer, *Saltwater Fishing: A Tactical Approach* provides it all. We focus on the best tips and tactics for fishing the beach, jetty, back bay, and inshore or offshore locations from either the beach or boat.

All of us, at one time or another, have met someone who has made a significant impact or impression on our lives when it comes to this sport, and it is our hope that *Saltwater Fishing: A Tactical Approach* will do the same for you. Within this book you will find a compilation of more than 100 years of fishing-related experience in northeastern waters, along with some excerpts and photos from our most in-depth previously published articles. We give you our best, no holds barred, no secrets left unturned. We welcome you along for the fishing-related experience of a lifetime, one that you can go back to over and over again. Let's go fishin'!

—Captain Jim, Captain Gene, and Shell E.

I

Jetty Fishing

1

Gearing Up for the Jetty

$\Large\mathsf{A}$long the eastern seaboard, the beaches of many municipalities are known for their jetty construction. In many locations, these rockpiles jut out every several hundred yards or so. These structures were originally constructed to trap any sand being transported by the littoral current, which moves parallel to the beach. This in turn would deposit sand on the beach, making it wider.

But for the most part, these structures have had a negative impact on reshaping beach profiles. Rather than deposition, we have seen beach erosion dominating this dynamic process. As a result, more and more beach is lost with every ensuing season. To reverse this process, the Army Corps of Engineers has undertaken a rather aggressive beach restoration program in several states.

While this restoration program is not without controversy, anglers can still look to jetties to provide an avenue to fish that ordinarily would be unreachable from the beach. Even when a restoration project along a particular stretch of beach is completed, Mother Nature has a way of undoing what humans have done. Over time jetty tips become reexposed and marine life and food chains reestablish themselves.

Incidentally, jetties are technically found at the mouths of inlets; all other rock structures along the beach are called groins, though fishermen rarely use this moniker.

JETTY SAFETY

As you begin to read our book, our time-proven techniques and tactics will unfold for you, and hopefully you will become a better fisherman because of it. But we need to stress that as much fun as catching fish can be, we are putting ourselves in the hands of Mother Nature each and every time we hit the beach, venture out in a boat, or explore a jetty.

We need to respect the awesome power of nature and of the sea. Needless to say, we have no control over these. Conditions can change quickly in the course of a day, and sometimes quick decisions will be necessary to stay out of precarious situations.

Personal safety must be paramount in our fishing. This means using our heads and not taking chances or risks that could jeopardize our safety or that of others.

Jetty safety begins before you set foot on a single rock. Your first judgment call is simply a matter of common sense: Venture out only on a jetty that is walkable. Some jetties have purposely been constructed with angler fishing in mind: Their rocks have been placed with their flat faces directed upward. These jetties are easy to walk on, although gaps between the rocks will still exist. Other jetties have been designed with their rocks placed irregularly; safe travel across them was not the intent of the engineers. Trying to scale the rocks of a jetty that has no flat faces is simply asking for trouble. There is a reason why some jetties have been named "suicide jetties" by the locals, so take notice.

Your second consideration is an awareness of wave height and period. *Wave period* is defined as the time required for each successive wave to pass a given point—in this case, your position on the rocks. Before you even venture out onto a jetty, observe the wave pattern striking the rocks for a good period of time, especially if there's any doubt in your mind that washovers may leave things unsafe. Also look for the development of any rogue waves.

Nighttime Considerations

Fishing a jetty at night is a completely different experience from the daytime, and once again safety should be your first consideration. If you do hit the rocks at night, choose a jetty that you are totally familiar with. Nighttime is not the time for exploring new locations. You should know exactly what rocks to stand on and where you can land a fish if you have to climb down the rocks toward the water. Trying to be a hero at night on the rocks is only asking for trouble. Familiarity with a jetty minimizes risk.

If you are venturing out alone at night, leave an itinerary with someone letting them know where and when you expect to be at different locations. Most importantly, give them a time when you expect to return home—and stick to it. Make sure you have a light and a cell phone with you; these may be the only ways you can communicate with someone if you get in trouble. We will explore fishing at night in more detail in chapter 16.

JETTY GEAR

Travel light. We have seen many anglers lug all sorts of gear and coolers out on the rocks, only to find out that none of it helped them catch fish. Stick to the basics. Traveling light will keep you most agile and allow you to free up your hands in case an unfortunate spill does occur.

Korkers

Foot apparel is critical. Jetties are extremely slippery when wet, because a thin layer of algae will cover most of the rocks. To make certain of sure footing, we recommend you wear a pair of Korkers over your boots at all times.

> ***Tip***
> Korkers will bite best when the jetty rocks are wet. You should still be extra careful, however, when stepping on any rocks that are angled upward or downward.

Korkers are a must for safety when fishing jetty rocks. Freda

Korkers are sandals studded with tungsten carbide steel. They're manufactured by Korkers in Clackamas, Oregon. Many different styles are available, some with laces, some with buckles and straps; there's even a full wading boot with interchangeable soles. The Konvertible Wading Boots with OmniTrax sole technology is the all-in-one boot. You can go from a spiked to a lug, felt, or even boat sole by quickly changing inserts. Check out www.korkers.com for the full product line and information.

If you've never worn a pair of Korkers, one of the keys is simply to relax when you're walking on the rocks and step as you would naturally. If you tense up your legs, that's when you'll get yourself into trouble. Your confidence level with the different feel underfoot will build with each step that you take. Korkers has been setting the safety standard in the industry for decades. Accept no substitute.

Surf Bags

A wide variety of surf bags is available to carry your plugs and artificials. Many bags have only one size insert and cannot accommodate large wooden swimmers. Select a bag that has both small and large inserts. Large wooden swimmers are a must in fall when big bunker are on the scene. Many times this is all the bass will take, so you don't want to be caught without them.

Only put your bag down on the rocks if there is no doubt in your mind that waves are not going to wash over the jetty. Most jetty jocks prefer to keep their bag shouldered at all times. This leads to an annoying problem, however: Each time you bend down to land a fish, your bag will slide forward from your hip to a position in front of you. This can occur over and over and be a real nuisance.

To solve this problem, you can wear a belt that loops through the back of the bag and then buckles around your waist. Drawn tight, this belt will hold the bag in place on your hip. It also keeps the bag from moving around when you travel from rock to rock.

The Great Debate: Bibs Versus Waders

Probably the most discussed topic when it comes to jetty attire is: Should you wear waders on a jetty? The ideal jetty attire will have you in bibs, knee-high boots, Korkers, and a rain jacket. Bibs—waterproof, bootless pants that cover you up to your chest—are better than waders because they are lighter, less restricting, and allow for more freedom of movement, a big safety advantage. Moving around on the rocks will feel more natural, and keeping your balance will come more easily.

If you plan to move from jetty to jetty, however, or fish the beach that lies between the two, then bibs are not the ideal attire. With bibs on, you will find that as you wade out into the surf, water runs up into your boots. The same thing happens when waves rush up the beach and pass through your legs.

In a case like this, you might want to wear waders. If you do choose to wear your bibs in the surf, however, we recommend cinching down the bottom of the pant legs with a Velcro strap. Pulling tight on this strap will keep out most of the water. If you have an older pairs of bibs, you can use a length of duct tape, wrapped tight around the pant legs, to do the same thing. You can add or remove the tape each time you go.

Our Shore Catch Grand Slam Fly School teaches all you need to know about beach and jetty safety. Freda

If you take a spill into the water with your waders on, you will quickly find out how difficult it is to swim when they fill up with water. If this does happen, try to remain calm. Panicking will only get you into more trouble. Waders that are filled with water will not pull you down.

Simply remove the waders while in the water. This will make getting out much easier.

Wearing a wading belt pulled tightly around your waist will slow the entry of water into a pair of boots but will not prevent the water from eventually filling them. It may, however, give you enough time to lift yourself up out of the water or pull yourself to safety. A wide strap belt will work best, so take your time when selecting one.

2

Jetty Knowledge: Success on the Rocks

Originally intended to prevent coastal erosion, jetties have become a haven for fishermen seeking the bounty that swims around their edges. Striped bass, bluefish, weakfish, fluke, and even false albacore can all be had at different times of year by any angler who works the rocks.

The allure of fishing a jetty has placed many surf fishermen in a different category from those who keep their feet firmly planted on the sand. *Jetty jock*, *hard-core*, and even *elitist* are among the titles that have been bestowed on them. But regardless of the signature, jetties are prime locations to catch trophy fish on a consistent basis. And even if you miss out on the trophies, there are plenty of smaller fish in the rich ecosystem that exists around each rockpile.

Still, fishing from a jetty is far more difficult than fishing from a beach or boat, or in a back bay. Obstacles here require special attention if you are to be successful at catching and landing fish while also remaining safe.

Your success will be linked first and foremost to how comfortable you feel on the rocks. Proper gear and footwear—as addressed in chapter 1—should be your first priority. Awareness of wave height and period is also crucial. Be cognizant of the amount of time you have between oncoming waves after you have made your cast. This will dictate the time that you will have to retrieve your artificial or work your

World-renowned fly fisher Bob Popovics gives the thumbs up to this jetty-caught 20-lb striper by Shore Catch client Jay Tenure at the North Jetty, Island Beach State Park. Freda

live bait before it is affected by the wave or its breaking against the rocks. This time will also be important if you need to climb down the rocks to land a fish (we'll discuss this in more detail later in this chapter).

The actual topography and length of any particular jetty will limit the number of anglers that can fish it effectively and safely. Thus it's important to have a plan if you want to be the first to fish that honey hole. This may require walking out on the rocks in the dark so you are in position at first light.

Let's look more closely at jetty topography.

JETTY TOPOGRAPHY

When looking at a jetty, the untrained eye can easily be fooled into thinking that the structure ends where its tip meets the water. This isn't true: Submerged rocks, many of which have been dislodged by powerful nor'easters and hurricanes, extend much farther out below the water. In some instances, an additional 75 to 100 feet of jetty can be hidden below.

At the seawardmost part of a jetty, a current runs parallel to the beach just beyond the surf zone. This current is referred to as the littoral current or littoral drift. It can travel at different velocities and is responsible for transporting sand along the beach. You might be familiar with this current from swimming: It will quickly push you down the beach from the spot where you entered the water.

Visually it is very difficult to identify this current when looking at the water unless an object such as a piece of driftwood is floating in it. In this case, you'll spot the lateral movement of the driftwood as it drifts in the current's direction.

> **Tip**
> Many jetties have been built around the remains of pilings that at one time supported docks or bulkheads. At the tip these pilings will extend above the rocks, while they're hidden just below the water's surface. If you're working a jetty tip with your boat, be careful not to run your prop into one.

The littoral current does not affect a jetty's rock formations them- selves—the energy associated with the current isn't dynamic enough. Still, it's forceful enough to push and shape the sand around the rocks, affecting the jetty's bottom contours significantly.

If the littoral current is moving from south to north along the beach, there will be a significant build-up of sand on the south side of the jetty, which acts as a natural barrier to the free transfer of sand along the beach. This will leave the north side of the jetty void of sand, and a deep hole will develop just off the north side of the tip. On the tip's

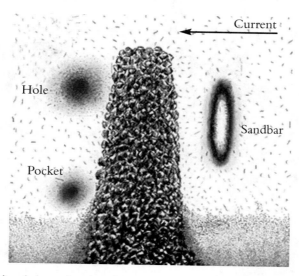

Fish-holding holes and pockets form on the side of a jetty opposite the current.

south side, a noticeable sandbar will develop as sand is deposited. As the sandbar builds, it will further prevent transported sand from refracting around the tip. The sand on the north side of the jetty will continue to slowly erode away because additional sand is not being deposited.

The north side of the rocks now becomes an ideal place for rip currents to form: Water moving out to sea will take the path of least resistance and flow along this side of the rocks. Further erosion will cause what is referred to as a pocket to form right where the water and sand meet. The pocket will take the shape of a bowl and usually deepens over time. The actual circumference of any particular pocket will vary from jetty to jetty. A sandbar will border most pockets on the side away from the jetty.

FISHING A JETTY'S POCKET

The pocket is one of the most productive fishing locations along the beach and should not be overlooked on any outing. Bait such as mullet, rainfish, peanut bunker, and spearing will get trapped here and become easy prey for bass and blues. At times the pocket will erupt, and the water will virtually boil with predators crashing through the baits.

Knowing when conditions like this will happen will be one of the keys to your success. Bait migrations occur in both spring and fall, which can put baits in the pocket at these times. Also, during summer months, baits can move inshore from their residential offshore grounds.

Look for the first day of a northeast storm for success on the rocks. Caris

Wind direction is usually the key factor dictating whether or not these baits will hold tight to the beach. Depending on your geographic location, certain winds will be favorable. Where we guide along the central New Jersey coast, a northeast wind pushes baits into the beach and traps them in jetty pockets.

Interestingly enough, we also see baits moving onto the beach when the winds blow out of the northwest. Such winds leave the water flat, and spotting baits becomes very easy. Some phenomenal blitzes have occurred on days of northwest winds.

FISHING A JETTY'S SIDES

All of our inshore target species will use rocks jetties to their advantage by trapping baits such as spearing, mullet, and bunker along the sides. Waves that break along the sides of the jetty rocks or at their tip will cause any baits that are present to become disoriented or stunned, making them an easy meal.

For this reason, it's important to work your artificials all the way back to the edge of the rocks. Do not abandon the final 2 or 3 feet of your retrieve by lifting your artificial out of the water. Keep moving your artificial slowly along. Another good tactic is to just hold your artificial in place along the sides of the rocks, allowing the current to produce undulations. Many times a bass or bluefish will have been tracking the artificial, waiting for this opportune moment to ambush it.

FISHING A JETTY'S TIP

One of the best locations on a jetty to consistently hook fish is its tip. Since there is much subsurface structure at this point, a prolific marine ecosystem will be established there, attracting both bait and predators.

In addition, downwardly sloping beach topography makes this area deeper than any other along the jetty. Large predators use this to their advantage as they lie in wait to ambush unsuspecting bait that is at or near the surface. It never ceases to amaze us how predators—particularly bass—can find injured or stunned baits in all the white foam generated when waves break on a jetty tip.

When you begin jetty fishing, a good rule of thumb is to fish the tip first, particularly at first light. This is usually where the largest fish will be located. This makes the tip an attractive place; it can become crowded quickly, especially if there is easy access and parking available.

> **Tip**
> If you're fishing a jetty tip during the day, and there's a lot
> of whitewater around the rocks, a dark plug or fly will pro-
> vide a good contrast. This may help the fish visually spot
> your artificial.

Fan out casts from the tip at many different angles. Conditions are
most favorable at high tide when the water is relatively calm, but there's
still some whitewater coming on. At low tide there may not be enough
water to retrieve your artificials without snagging the rocks below.

In rough water, a tip may be unfishable due to large waves breaking
on top of it or pouring large volumes of whitewater upon its face. If you
underestimate the potential of an oncoming swell, you can easily be
swept off your feet. In questionable situations, it's better to err on the
side of safety and remain back from the tip.

FLY FISHING FROM JETTIES

If you're fly fishing a jetty, it's crucial to note what your line is doing
immediately after a cast. This is that brief transition time when you position your rod and hands in order to begin stripping. After the cast, many
fly fishers will immediately focus on stripping to catch a fish. It is, however, during this transition time that your line can become hopelessly
entangled in the jetty rocks or swept away by encroaching waves. There
is a mental checklist that each fly fisher should go through immediately
after the cast, in order to manage the line properly. Certain conditions
make the problem worse, and while an awareness of these conditions is
necessary, it is usually learned through experience, for many of us such
awareness comes only after a line is lost and the damage is done. If you're
a budget-conscious fly fisher, a lost line can put you in a hole even
before a fish has put a bend in your rod.

The first problem to watch out for is losing line from your stripping basket. The wind is usually the nemesis here. As you begin to strip,
a head-on or crossing wind can push your line over the side of the
basket and drop it to the rocks below. At this point, each successive strip
into the basket will be pulled out by the weight of the line hanging out
of it. By the time you realize what is happening, a good amount of line
will already be in the rocks.

To prevent this, make sure your first couple of coils are lying flat in the bottom of the basket around its inserts. You can do this by allowing your hand to touch the bottom of the basket on your first series of strips, rather than just letting go of the line from several inches above the basket bottom.

Changing to a wider and deeper basket will also help. And as simple as it may sound, one of your best preventive measures is to take a look to see that the line is in your basket and not falling out.

When crossing winds are the culprit, you can also move your stripping basket slightly to the downwind side of your body. This will allow your body to act as a natural barrier or shield that the wind will have to diffract around. As a result, the airflow around your basket will be minimized. If you're used to stripping line directly in front of you and don't like the feel of stripping to the side, try repositioning your entire body to block the wind as an alternative.

> **Tip**
>
> When fly fishing from a jetty with long leaders, taper them down from a heavier section of 30-pound test to 20-pound test. This heavier butt section will give you added protection from a break-off if a hooked fish decides to run across the rocks. Also, this heavier section will allow you to grab your leader to lift the fish onto the rocks. It's much more forgiving to your hands than a lighter leader.

If your line does get caught in the rocks, don't try to retrieve it by pulling from the back of the line, near the reel. Pulling on this end of the hanging loop will just bury the line more deeply in the rocks. It will also pull your line across any mussels or barnacles that may be present. These will act like tiny little razors and fray the line. Rather, if safety permits, try to grab the front part of the line loop just below the first stripping guide. Position yourself over the spot where the line is caught and pull upward on the line as you work it back toward you. This pulls the line over and away from the rocks rather than through them.

Oncoming waves can also pull line out of your basket after a cast. Even if there is no wind, oncoming waves can still be present as wave energy reaches the jetty rocks from prior offshore wind events.

Oncoming waves can particularly wreak havoc if your eyes are focused on only the part of your line that's in the water out in front of the tip.

From a jetty, your height above the water's surface will often produce a belly in the line that extends from your rod tip to the water. The higher up you are, the more line belly there will be. You should also notice that as you lower your rod from the final casting position to your stripping position, your line will drop straight down. During this repositioning time, one wave is all it will take to sweep your line back into the rocks. This is particularly true on rough days when waves and whitewater keep rolling in.

The solution rests in part in simply being cognizant of what this section of line is doing as you prepare to strip. It will take a few more seconds to position your reel under and just behind your armpit for a two-handed strip than it does to begin a single-handed retrieve. In both cases, however, hand speed in maneuvering your rod into position to strip, along with developing good hand–eye coordination to help you find your line, are important.

It's also important to quickly come tight to your fly. This will remove any slack or belly from your line and give you more line control while eliminating any chance of line being pulled from your basket by sweeping waves.

Another helpful technique is learning to time incoming waves or pushes of whitewater as they move past you. Once you can do this, you'll be able to throw a cast so that it lands on the back side of a wave and not in front of it. You can also throw a mend into your line over that first oncoming wave, lifting and placing your line on the back side of the wave. Both of these techniques will give you more time to pick up your slack and to get ready to strip.

If you're fishing a quick-sinking line, the belly of the line that extends out beyond your rod tip poses an additional problem: More wait time is needed for your line to sink to the depth you're looking for. Water hitting the belly at this point will pull your line back or keep it from sinking to where you want it to be.

To manage your line in this case, hold your rod tip high immediately following your cast. This will keep your line up off the water and eliminate any drag that may result from an oncoming wave. As your line is sinking, begin to slowly lower your rod tip while extending your arm slightly outward. This will allow more line to be taken below the surface. If a current is moving your line, you'll need to feed line from your reel while holding your rod tip out.

Finally, be aware that one fly fisher can take up the same amount of space on a jetty that would normally hold three or even four spin casters. This is due to the additional room needed for backcasts. We recommend being courteous to your fellow anglers when you are out on the rocks with the long rod. This often means giving up your space to them, even if you were out there first. Having arguments develop over space considerations is not what this sport is all about. A little consideration goes a long way.

For more about fly fishing, see chapter 17.

FIGHTING AND LANDING FISH

Special consideration needs to be giving to fighting fish from a jetty, because you'll be moving around a lot during the ensuing battle. You need to be focused on not only what the fish is doing but also what your feet are doing. It will be important to maintain both your balance and control of the fish's head as you move around.

Applying side pressure to a fish's head is a good control technique. A rod that is angled slightly above parallel to the water will apply more pressure than a rod held vertically, which means less time spent subduing your fish. You're less likely to play it to exhaustion, increasing its chances of survival when released.

Adjusting your rod position is important if and when a fish runs on you. If the fish runs to your right, turn your rod to the left, and vice versa. This will help you maintain head control and also drive the hook more deeply into the fish's mouth.

It is best to have a landing strategy already mapped out in your mind even before a fish is actually hooked. Look for a set of flat rocks near the water's edge or any covelike indentation that you can easily climb down to. If possible, select a rock that your fish can be led and slid onto; then net or gaff it from this location. Most small fish can be landed this way.

If you're trying to land a trophy fish, more than likely you will need to get off the rocks. Walking a fish off the rocks and landing it in the surf is safer than climbing down the rocks and trying to lift the lunker up. And after you've successfully walked a fish off the rocks, *don't* immediately begin reeling it in while still standing next to the jetty. To eliminate any chance of the fish running back into the rocks, walk a good distance away from them before you begin your retrieve. Keep constant pressure on the fish while you do this, not allowing any slack to develop in your line.

Releasing a fish from a jetty can pose a problem if reviving the fish is difficult due to your location on the rocks and oncoming waves. Once again, you must consider your personal safety. A better plan is to move closer to the beach, where wave action against the rocks is minimized.

Many times fish—particularly small ones—can be tossed back into the water headfirst and will do just fine. When released this way, water will rush through their mouths and over their gills, reviving them more quickly. You'll want to take care, however, with larger fish. Look for a location on the side of the jetty opposite the waves to revive your fish before releasing it.

PART

II

Beach Fishing

3

Hit the
Beach

Surf fishing has attracted many people, young and old, to the sport of saltwater fishing. Perhaps it's because of the surf's beauty and serenity, or its easy access. Whatever the reason, there's nothing more satisfying than making a cast in the surf and catching a hard-pulling predator.

READING BEACH STRUCTURE

One of the most difficult tasks for most surf anglers is reading the beach. At first glance, the surf looks the same in each direction. To the experi-

Shore Catch Guide Darin Muly and client Ed Cervone show why fly fishing the surf is fun for all ages. Freda

enced surf angler, however—whether fly, spin, or bait—the reality is quite the contrary.

Fishing success depends on locating beach structure and using it to your advantage. When anglers talk about reading the beach, they are referring to interpreting the appearance of the entire surf spectrum. Sunken rocks, sandbars, cuts, and points are just a few of the important structures you will encounter. Locating and understanding how these structures play a role in shelter and the underwater lifestyles of predators and bait alike will give you a decisive advantage.

When walking down a beach or driving it in your beach buggy, make mental notes along the way. Try to identify what is fishable now and what will be fishable later. Knowing as much as possible about the surf's structure in your area is the key to making predictions about how it will change throughout the tide. The easiest time to locate prime beach structure is during low tide. Sandbars, sloughs, cuts, and deep holes will be most visible during this period. Plug, fly, and bait anglers should learn all the different characteristics and opportunities of their respective shorelines.

Sandbars

The shoreline is constantly changing due to oncoming swells, changing winds, and tides. These conditions rearrange surf structures on a constant basis. Sandbars are one of the most important forms of beach structure because cuts, breaks, and deep holes form around or near them. Sandbars and the other structures around them are attractive to baitfish, crustaceans, clams, sand bugs, and worms because they offer protection and food.

One of the most challenging things about reading sandbars are that they are not fixed to one permanent position, but always shifting. Underwater sandbars can be located by reading the breaking waves. Whitewater generally indicates where a bar is located. Waves will break over bars and dump water into the area in front, known as a trough. The edge where the bar meets the trough is where predators hunt and prey fish hide.

A sandbar's value is based on its location and how it is situated in conjunction with the beach. As tidal changes occur, huge masses of water are either flowing or ebbing from the beach structures. This process can create a rip current that striped bass love. A rip is simply two opposing currents joining that then pull forcefully. Small baitfish will struggle and be swept through these rips, making them prime areas for anglers.

In many instances, two sandbars or a series of sandbars will form shifting pockets and holes as tides and conditions change. Baitfish will take up temporary residence from area to area, and these pathways create feeding stations for all types of gamefish. Stripers and other predators will spend a great deal of time in shallow water in search of these bait-fish, and the more time you can spend at the beach making observations about the conditions, the better you'll be able to recognize opportune times and places to fish.

All anglers should learn various stages of the tides in conjunction with the particular structures they're interested in fishing. After you've become familiar with the beach landscape, you'll notice that fish activity during the last hours of the bottom ebb tide may seem to rise because the hiding places disappear, leaving bait in open holes. The first few hours of an incoming tide are also a great time to fish, because these exposed baits are driven to find hiding spaces away from the grasp of hungry predators. Evening and night hours are especially productive, because predatory instincts rise as light fades. During these times, fish the holes, ledges, and the drop-offs around sandbars with flies and plugs for the best results.

Aerial view of a cut between two sand bars. Cuts are avenues for baitfish and predators.
Studio 9 Photo, Waretown

As water pushes over the bars into the troughs and holes, it will flow back out from the shoreline to create channels called cuts or breaks. Stripers, bluefish, and weakfish sit in these areas and wait for food to come to them as the overabundance of water flows to the open sea. Watch the breaking waves and pay attention to the direction of the current flow. Then think about how these flows are likely to route the baitfish.

> **Tip**
> Gamefish most often feed with their faces in the current, so cast your lures or flies upcurrent and work them toward the strike zone.

The best way to start your fishing is to visually explore the surf from the highest points available on the beach. Start casting on the sandbar, swimming your offering off the edge and into the deeper water. Try to mimic the disarrayed swimming patterns of helpless baitfish. Once your plug or fly is out of the strike zone, reel or strip in quickly and cast again. This will put your presentation fly back in the strike zone where fish are focused. Gamefish can be selective eaters, but once they're focused on a particular bait type they will often hit anything resembling it. Your assortment of flies, lures, or baits should represent what is available during the particular time of year. Therefore, knowing what species of baits are available through the seasons will greatly improve your results.

Sloughs

The best sloughs to fish are those running parallel to the beach. These troughs of deep water that form between beach and bar again offer significant feeding opportunities simply due to the change from shallow to deep water. Awesome events can take place in structures like these during fall migrations. Thousands of peanut bunker migrating south, for example, will often become trapped in the many sloughs along the surf line. As they try to escape, stripers and bluefish will ball the bait and attack. Such blitzes can continue all-out for hours, or can last mere minutes depending on the feeding behavior and amount of bait. Witnessing blitzes can be breathtaking, but unfortunately they don't happen every day. It's a good idea to fish deep sloughs and troughs whether you see anything or not: Gamefish will roam these huge pools of calm water throughout the season and throughout different periods of the tide, searching for food.

Anglers who fish flies and artificial lures should focus their efforts on the lower stages of the outgoing and incoming tides when fishing a slough, while bait fishers tend to prefer the higher portions of the moving tide. Remember, seasons influence fish behavior and feeding habits; you must adapt accordingly. In addition, having a general idea of water temperature and clarity will make choosing the proper lure or bait easier. This is not a direct science, however. One message that we always try to instill in our clients' minds is "Fish when you can, and don't over-look an area just because the conditions don't seem right." We have seen many anglers fishing the surf at the most inopportune times, only to catch the fish of a lifetime when the conditions weren't "right."

Points

Like sandbars, points are important forms of beach structure, and are often directly associated with sandbars as well as with long, drawn-out cresting breakers. Points are important to surfbound anglers because they form sharp structures that baitfish must traverse during both incoming and outgoing tides. Locating points on a small scale from boat, truck, or foot is simple: Just look down the scalloped coastline for the steep sand. This is easiest during low water. Points that develop on

Aerial view of a scalloped shoreline showing a point. Studio 9 Photo, Waretown

beaches generally have deeper water on one or both sides known as
bowls (discussed in the next section).

On a large scale, there are some very famous points along the East
Coast: Sandy Hook, New Jersey; Montauk Point, Long Island; "The
Point" at Hatteras, North Carolina; and Race Point on Cape Cod are
just a few that eastern anglers journey to every season. Not every point
along the East Coast is as large or well known, of course, and it's wise
to learn the smaller points along your own coastline.

When fishing points, make your cast in the area upcurrent and
work it toward the drop-off. Also, fan your casts so you cover the entire
area around the point. Sometimes fish will be competing for the area
right on the point itself. Be a prospector. After identifying where fish are
feeding around the point, take note of tide, wind, and time of day. As
long as there are no significant changes to these factors, you have gotten
a grasp of the feeding pattern for the week and can come back an hour
later the next day (taking account of tides) and score.

Bowls

Bowls are deep holes in the surf line that offer fish a semistable sanc-
tuary. Hard-hitting nearshore breakers can be associated with bowls.
However, the depth of bowls can vary from one to the next. When
looking at the sandbar–bowl relationship, it is important to know and
understand how and why waves break. As swells push in from the sea,
they travel over deep open water. As they approach the shore, they will
"peak" or "jack" when met with water that's shallower than the actual
wave height. These generally are sandbars or shallow upliftings on sand.
The wave's energy will force the wave to break over the bar, creating a
rumbling force of whitewater. The waves immediately lose momentum
once they have broken, thus petering out over the bowl, which turns

> *Tip*
> No matter how you're fishing the surf—from boat, beach
> or jetty—try to cast to the top crest of a crashing wave and
> let the fly or plug crash down with the wave. This is the
> most effective way to simulate natural baitfish behavior.
> Predators looking for the opportunity to feed will be
> transfixed on helpless bait in turmoil.

into a sort of collection area for many types of bait. Experienced surf anglers who use clams will find these areas attractive because clams and broken clamshells will gather in deeper bowls after storms.

Ledges

Ledges hold not only stripers, but also weakfish, bluefish, and other gamefish. They are among the richest fishing grounds available and are found near inlets, back bays, and along the coast. The ledge of a channel can run a long distance; if one location doesn't pay off, move to another.

Although feeding gamefish can often be found on the surface, sometimes predators seem more eager to strike down below, so concentrate on the bottom third of the water column. East Coast ledges can be giant drop-offs, but for inshore striper anglers working areas with very little structure, even the smallest ledges can be important places to cast.

> *Tip*
> Casting behind crashing whitewater is also an effective way to work your lure or fly. Striped bass and other predators frequently attack frazzled bait in our around the white suds.

Jetty Pockets

Among the most important areas along the beach are jetty pockets. Since pockets are almost unapproachable by boats, they are excellent spots for jetty and surf anglers. When all-out blitzes are taking place here, the fishing can be downright ridiculous—nearly a fish on every cast. Chapter 2, Jetty Knowledge, includes a section telling you everything you need to know about these hot spots.

TIDES

The ebb and flow of water affects every structure and living organism in the surf. Baitfish, like other species, roam the waters looking for shelter. They do not have a home per se, but they do have areas of preference. They forever seek food and shelter, and are in constant turmoil from the change of the environments in which they live. Safety from predators comes in large numbers and in the shallows. Deep holes, drop-offs, ledges, and rock structures are just a few other sanctuaries for baitfish. Gamefish know the currents and conditions of their environments, including currents that sweep bait into danger zones, and make better use of them than the hiding baitfish.

When fishing these coastal waters, your greatest concern as an angler is not what time the water is high or low. *High tide* refers only to the point at which water reaches its highest level at that stage; the same holds true for low tide. Instead, you should be aware of the point at which the current stops moving and becomes slack. Water will slacken during the short time before it changes directions from incoming or outgoing. This can be a prime time to fish.

4

Natural Baits: Technical Presentation

Fishing natural baits from the beach is a virtually guaranteed way to succeed. As stripers, blues, or weakfish move through the surf zone, they will key in on the natural baits indigenous to a particular locale. A wide variety of invertebrate species and baitfish can make up the bulk of their diet.

In our guiding area, several natural baits have proven highly effective when fished with the correct technical presentation: sea worms, sea clams, and cut baits.

Technical presentation refers to the proper way to rig a natural bait and the best time of the season to fish it. Proper terminal tackle and tying methods enable you to present a common bait in the most natural way possible. Although bass and other gamefish at times become opportunistic and take unlikely baits in unlikely ways, better success rates will come to those who pay attention to detail.

WORMS

Although sea clams have become the natural bait of choice along the eastern seaboard, many veteran striped bass anglers still know the importance of natural sea worms for catching fish. Worms are sold all along the East Coast as bait for almost any saltwater species, though they're most often used by flounder and striped bass anglers in early spring.

Blood worms are best fished during the spring months. These baits were popular in the 1970s, but the trend changed and sand worms are by far the preferred bait along northeastern shores today. In comparison, blood worms are generally found on mudflats and can be dug during low tides. Use a curved pitchfork to pull the mud toward you; this will expose the worms. Healthy worms are firm with a red to pinkish coloration.

Sand worms are usually found and dug in the darker, gravelly sand of tidal rivers. Prime locations can be near pilings or bulkheads, and along riverbanks during dead low tide. These worms have a blue-green tint and can be up to 12 inches long. After exposing them, keep them in the drier sand in the same area that they were dug. Here they will secrete some fluid and firm up.

Both of these worms can be purchased over the counter by the dozen or by the flat. Common tackle for rigging includes the pompano rig, better known as the high/low rig. Our recommendation, however, is to use the fishfinder rig with two 1/0 to 3/0 snelled baitholder hooks on a 24-inch leader. Also, an optional torpedo-style float can be used to keep the worms off the bottom. The proper hooking method is to pierce the mouth through the hard head section then push the worm up the hook so the barbs hold it in place. This method presents the worm as naturally seen by a predator.

Another natural forage is the green sea worm. These worms are opaque, pale green in color, but are not as durable as the blood or sand worm. They can, however, be fished all season long. You can obtain a good supply for a day's fishing by using a pitchfork on sandbars or in very shallow areas in small pools of water.

Shell E.'s dad introduced him to these treasured worms back in the early 1960s. One of his weekly chores was to dig worms for his dad's weekend fishing trips; in return, he would receive his allowance. Unlike store-bought worms, which are refrigerated in moist seaweed, beach worms should be stored in a 5-gallon pail of ocean water and kept cool. Water should be changed daily. With this method, you'll be able to keep a good supply of worms alive for a week in a large refrigerator.

> **Tip**
> When digging green worms in the surf, if you run across large numbers of small worms—an inch or less—move to a different location. The larger worms are usually found away from the small ones.

These worms are an irresistible bait and will outproduce blood and sand worms in any given situation. Remember, the largest baits do not necessarily catch the largest stripers. With worms, it is more important to make sure they are fresh and firm. Worms of such quality will remain on the hook the longest and undulate the most temptingly as they sit on the bottom.

CLAMS

Among the most abundant and popular natural baits along the Northeast Coast are hard sea clams, commonly referred to as surf clams (*Spisula solidissima*). These are some of the largest clams that can be found washed up along the eastern seaboard, particularly after a northeast storm. They can reach a diameter of 6 inches. Their umbo—the point of their bivalve shell—is at the top center of the shell proper.

It's also worth looking for the quahog (*Mercenaria mercenaria*), Rhode Island's state shell. The bivalve point of this shell is off center. Native Americans used quahog shells to make the beads they used as money (wampum).

In most states it is illegal to take clams from the beach without a clamming license. They can, however, be purchased from your local tackle shop; commercial draggers keep the stores stocked. Prices will vary with supply.

> ### Tip
> Put fresh clams in a plastic airtight container filled with seawater and freeze. When defrosted, the clams will be as firm and fresh as unfrozen clams.

Fresh clams are by far the most productive, although many striped bass have inhaled old ones. If fresh clams cannot be obtained, use frozen or salted. We prefer to use the entire clam, including the tongue and the ribbons. This is the most natural presentation and will get you the best results.

The most common and most effective rig for fishing clams is the nylon fishfinder rig. These come prerigged with a baitholder hook and can be purchased over the counter. Hook sizes will usually range from 3/0 through 7/0. The fishfinder rig attaches above the barrel swivel that connects your leader to your hook. It's essentially a small nylon sleeve that slides freely over your main running line. There is a clip on the sleeve where your weight is attached. The design of this rig will allow a bass to pick up your clam and swim away without detecting any resistance from the weight. Fresh clams do not need to be secured; they will stay on the hook. If need be, however, we use elastic thread, available at tackle shops.

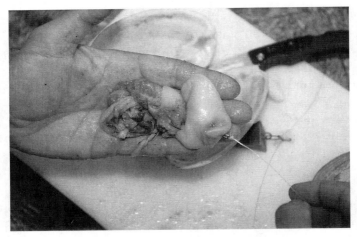

Natural sea clams have become one of the most popular baits for striped bass. Use a fresh whole clam. Caris

You can catch fish on clams all season long, but some of the best action will occur during storms, especially nor'easters. During a storm, sea clams are uprooted from their beds by strong currents and wave action. They get pushed toward the shoreline, where they tumble and break up. A natural chum slick and clam wash is produced, which will draw stripers in tight to the beach and trigger some great fishing.

CUT MACKEREL

Another excellent natural bait to consider in spring is fresh mackerel. This forgotten bait was once the one of surf fishing's most popular, producing more huge bass than any other bait during its time. Back in the 1960s and '70s, bait shops would stock fresh unfrozen mackerel. Many shops today do not offer these baits because the schools have not come close enough to the beach in the recent years.

Mackerel, however, remain very effective in spring. It is not uncommon for mackerel anglers on party boats to hook into a big bass. Most likely the bass went after the mackerel and got hooked.

We usually see mackerel schools migrating north through our New Jersey waters in late April anywhere from 5 to 15 miles off the beach. Right on their heels will be striped bass as well as the first bluefish of the season. The window of opportunity for these baits is slim, however—only a few weeks. A spring storm can hasten the migration window and drive these baits even farther offshore.

Mackerel are a very oily bait. The key to fishing them is to have them fresh, not frozen. To prepare a mackerel fillet, neatly cut a side slab into a triangular wedge. You can experiment with varying lengths and widths. The bait can be rigged in several ways. You can use a fishfinder rig with a float, a pompano rig, or a tandem fishfinder rig.

With a fishfinder rig, add a torpedo-style float to give the mackerel a dancing, undulating action. This will produce a fresh scent from the bait that will disperse underwater and be of interest to bass and other predators.

Since fresh mackerel can be difficult to obtain at a bait shop, try going to the docks and buying a handful when the party boats come in from their runs. For a few dollars, you could have all you need for a day or two of fishing. When these baits are accessible, it's worth making the effort to fish them—they are the forgotten dream bait!

BUNKER HEADS

All veteran bass anglers know the importance of adult menhaden, or bunker. Although we prefer to use them live, we also have tremendous success fishing cut bunker, especially the heads. This large offering produces trophy bass every season.

This type of bait fishing was a favorite of some of our friends in the Long Beach Island area. Year after year, cow-sized bass fell to this method. It's now very popular up and down the coast, especially in New Jersey's Ocean and Monmouth Counties.

Tip
When using cut bunker, scale the bunker to release more of the fish oils.

The most popular rig for bunker heads is the common fishfinder rig. Attach the nylon sleeve to the running line, and then add a 230-pound-test Spro barrel swivel to tie your leader to. The leader should be 40- to 50-pound test and 8 to 12 inches long. Such a short leader enables you to cast farther and easier, eliminating the helicopter effect you get with a long leader.

When a bass inhales a head, it will be in the mouth completely; setting the hook on the take will help prevent gut-hooking. And if you see your rod twitching or getting bumped slightly after the bait is set, it may be because crabs are tucking away at it. Check your baits regularly.

CALICO CRABS

Calico crabs are best fished from June through August and are a bait that will always produce fish when all others fail. During the summer of 1953 Shell, then age seven, was introduced to these baits when his father took him surf fishing. His dad was an avid striped bass angler and used calico crabs exclusively. He called them "the miracle bait."

Shell recalls what happened: "My family were natives of Newark, New Jersey, but we had a summer home in Belmar. One hot summer night my father took me with him to the Eighth Avenue Jetty to do some crab fishing for stripers. I remember that day like it was yesterday.

Calico crabs are preyed upon by almost every local species. Secure them to the hook with elastic thread. Caris

My fishing rod was an 8-foot Calcutta matched to a Penn 155 reel spooled with 36-pound Dacron line. We positioned ourselves next to the south side of the jetty during the outgoing tide.

"My dad had an old cigar box filled with about a dozen calicos in it. The crabs were covered with a piece of moist newspaper to keep them fresh. Dad picked up one of those crabs out of the box and said, 'This should be a fish.'

"What he was saying was, if a bass is around, you're going to catch it! The crab he pulled out was very soft. He said, 'Stripers love softies.' My dad put the soft calico crab on a 5/0 hook using sewing machine cotton thread and wrapped the hook to it. When he was done, he made a cast with my rod just past the first wave. He then handed me the rod and said, 'Hold on tight.'

"Within minutes I felt a tremendous tug; I hooked, fought, and landed my first striper, a sweet 7-pound fish! I will never forget it. I was hooked on striper fishing for life."

Calico crabs are caught by raking the surf with what's called a calico rake. When raking, you will be looking for calicos in specific stages of their life cycle. The crabs you want to gather are the softies, shedders, and tin backs. Identifying these stages will take some practice.

Soft-shell crabs are easy to identify: Their bodies are totally limp and soft. Shedders and peelers are identified by color. As molting occurs, the new shell will begin to form and become visible from underneath the hardening shell. Male shedders have a pronounced lavender color on the bottom claw.

The last stage of the peeler is identified not by color but a physical condition of the hard shell. A split develops under the lateral spines and along the posterior edge of the shell. At this stage, the crab is called a buster; it has begun molting and backs out of its shell. This is a very soft prime bait for striped bass. As the calicos begin to turn hard in this early stage, they are called tin backs or tinees. They, too, are very productive baits.

Begin raking two hours before low tide. Look for pockets of soft sand along the beach, as well as working the areas along the north and south sides of the jetties. The best times for raking calico crabs are during new- and full-moon phases.

To fish calicoes, we prefer to use conventional tackle and an 8-foot medium-action rod. This outfit is spooled with 20-pound-test mono or 50-pound braid. Again, the most popular rig for using calico crabs is the fishfinder rig. We recommend using number 2017 Octopus–style 710 Gamakatsu hooks, which are chemically sharpened.

Lay the hook along the underside of the crab and tie the hook to the crab body with elastic cotton thread or spider thread. Spider thread is almost invisible. By tying the crabs' legs along the leader, the bait will be presented naturally.

5

Fall Bonanza on the Beach

Every angler's dream is to go down to the surf and walk right into a major blitz of bass or blues. If you're on the water enough, this will happen to you. There will be mornings when bass are busting right at your feet, and days when blues will come in with the high water to provide nonstop action. These are indeed exciting times, but if you are a once-in-a-while day-tripper, chances are you will be reading about the action in the next day's newspaper or on an Internet message board.

October is prime time for blitzes of bass and blues along the beach. Freda

FISHING THE BLITZES

Blitzes of stripers, blues, and false albacore do occur all along the Atlantic seaboard and are controlled by a number of factors. Tides, weather, surf conditions, lunar phases, time of day, and much more can all come into play. The two key factors, however, are water temperatures and the presence of bait.

The majority of our striped bass, bluefish, and false albacore blitzes occur in fall when baits are prevalent and ocean temperatures are dropping. Mullet, spearing, bay anchovies, peanut bunker, adult bunker, sand eels, and sea herring are some of the main baits that drive Atlantic blitzes. Each is present at a different time during fall, though some overlap takes place.

Dropping water temperatures start bait moving from north to south and as a result draw the above three gamefish to feed. Since the bass, blues, and albies are also preparing to move south for the winter, they will gorge themselves to increase their energy reserves; all-out blitzes can occur.

Webster's defines *blitz* as a "sudden, destructive, or overwhelming attack." In the ocean this would be an all-out assault of predator on prey. Blitzes are quite a sight, and you don't have to be a fishing person to appreciate one. The sheer numbers of bait and fish that can be present in a small area are usually mind boggling. Sometimes it looks as if Mount Vesuvius were erupting below the water.

Blitzes can be all-day events, from sunrise to sunset. On days like these, one hookup after another is common. Each cast gets you another fish. During the fall of 2003, blitzes were common along the New Jersey beaches as thousands upon thousands of peanut bunker were in the surf and along the jetties. Here is an excerpt from one of the daily reports posted on our Web site, www.shorecatch.com:

> The action today was nothing short of phenomenal as teen-sized bass and blues had the peanut bunker pinned to the jetty for most of the day. "If I made forty casts I had forty fish," commented one angler. And another: "I've been fishing the beach for over forty years and have never seen it this good. It's insane."

In New Jersey, the North Jetty at Island Beach State Park is well known as a blitz location. This is attributed to the jetty's length—it sticks out into the ocean for several hundred yards. When the bait is present and conditions are right, it can be an explosive place to be. Fly fishers in particular have traveled from the tristate area to set up on the North Jetty during the peak of the false albacore run to try to catch one of these prized speedsters.

> **Tip**
> Blue Water Designs of Bristol, Connecticut (www.bluewa-ternet.com), make a wide range of prerigged wire shock tippets for both fly and spin fishing. These can quickly and easily be tied to your leader when bluefish are on the scene.

You can predict when a blitz will occur with higher probability if you're familiar with the timing of when particular baits show up in your area. Often bait migrations are initiated by lunar phases and accelerated by dropping water temperatures; a knowledge of these factors will only help keep you on top of the fishing.

In our guiding area, for example, we see mullet moving along the beach in September; bay anchovies, spearing, and bunkers mainly in October and early November; and sand eels and sea herring from mid November through late December. On the full and new moons in September, a push of mullet will occur along the beach. And if nighttime temperatures in late October drop down into the 20s for several days, a push of peanut bunker will come out of the back bays. We can plan our fishing around these events.

Other autumn conditions are also worth keeping track of. When an approaching low-pressure northeast system is coming up the coast, for instance, hit the surf on the storm's first day. This is when the action can erupt into a classic blitz.

There are several reasons why we look to the first day of a multiday storm event to be the most productive. First, bass and blues are in a feeding mode and on high alert to anything in their surroundings that will provide or enhance feeding opportunities.

As the winds turn or move onshore, this will produce a lot of wave action and whitewater, pushing the fish into the beaches or jetties. Such rough water will trap and disorient the bait, making it an easy meal for

> **Tip**
> Mullet have a tendency to swim near the upper part of the water column and seem to always be moving along. For this reason, use a steady retrieve when working your artificials around a school. If you're fly fishing, employ a steady two-handed retrieve rather than a strip–pause type of retrieve.

a predator on the prowl. Bass and blues will make the most of conditions like these.

Conditions on the first day of an extended blow can be exactly what stimulates fish to feed and congregate along the beach. By the second or third day of the event, however, the water can be too rough or turbid to fish effectively. Wave heights can increase drastically, which will push too much whitewater toward the beach and make effective retrieves impossible. Or the water can get so churned up with suspended sand that it is off color and looks dirty. Strong winds and rains can also make for some rather uncomfortable conditions.

Bob's Bangers are ideal surface fleyes for scoring big blues in a surface blitz. Freda

FEEDING FRENZIES

If you're out on the water enough, your blitz days will come. Your timing will be right, the conditions will be right, and the bait and fish will be there. Sometimes, however, you can be in the right place at the right time with fish blitzing right in front of you—yet you're not catching anything. The frustration can build rather quickly.

Typically what you are faced with is a feeding frenzy, and the bass or blues are keyed in on the scent of the baits as they get chopped up in the melee. If this happens to you, there are several strategies that you can employ to entice fish to strike:

- When fish are keyed in on the real baits, you can fish an artificial that features a marked difference in size and profile. This unusual artificial will draw attention to itself, and fish may strike out at it out of aggression.
- You can use an artificial that will sink down below the bait school. This will mimic an injured bait that can no longer maintain its position in the upper part of the water column. Injured baits are easy meals for predators. Many times bass will wait below bait schools for chunks to drop down to them after bluefish have chomped them on the surface.
- You can fish to the sides of the blitzing pod. Some fish will stay outside the main body, looking for an opportunity to grab a bait.
- You can remain in place and fish behind a pod of blitzing fish after it has moved on down the beach instead of chasing the bait and fish, as many fishermen will do. Staying in place will give you an opportunity at much larger fish as they move behind the main school feeding on the injured baits that have been left behind. Striped bass in particular exhibit this type of behavior as a way to conserve energy.
- Consider fishing on the surface with a topwater artificial that will make a lot of commotion. Large splashes will get the attention of predators rather quickly, and—just as with an unusual bait—the gamefish will strike out of aggression as their territory is being encroached upon.
- Lastly, you can allow your artificial to just dead drift or remain motionless in all the melee. This is a very effective technique, because your artificial appears to be stunned, seemingly an easy meal. Doing this, however, is easier said than done given all the adrenaline surging through your body during the heat of a blitz. For this reason it's a method that's rarely employed by anglers—but should be.

> **Tip**
> A plain old-fashioned white bucktail makes an excellent artificial to fish below pods of blitzing fish. This jig will sink quickly through the school, and the wide profile that bucktail's buoyant nature provides will serve to attract fish.

THE BEACH BUGGY ADVANTAGE

When blitzes are occurring, fish commonly push the bait down the beach. Many times bass and blues will stay with a particular pod of bait as they indiscriminately shoot in and out of the school, feeding to their hearts' content. When the baits are on the move, many times you will need to be also if remaining in place does not produce any results.

Here is where a beach buggy, a 4×4 vehicle, will keep you right on top of the action. Many municipalities along the Atlantic seaboard allow 4×4 beach buggy access during certain times of year—usually in spring before the summer beach season begins, and in fall after it's over. Some spots, like Island Beach State Park in New Jersey, provide access year-round.

Having a 4×4 vehicle on the beach will increase your productivity and in many cases your enjoyment. It's similar to having a boat in the water: You can use the vehicle to move quickly from place to place, surveying the ocean as you go. If you spot any action, you can pull right up to it just as you would if you were in a boat. Anything you can do to save time means more time that your offering will be in the water.

In a blitz, if the bait is on the move, you can drive ahead of the moving school and get set up as the bait and fish come right to you. Often this will put you ahead of the crowds, too, and you can then pick and choose when you will make your cast.

Having the vehicle means you won't have to lug gear along on your person. Everything you carry can stay right in your truck until you need it. You also have the option of carrying a wider variety of equipment that you wouldn't be able to bring otherwise.

Rigging your vehicle with multiple rod holders will give you a place to put your rod to keep it out of the sand. If you need to change a plug or retie a rig, you can use your truck as a platform to work out of. Often if you're trying to retie a leader when down on the sand, there's no place to put your rod safely as your work at or near the tip. This is especially true if you have to reline through all your guides. With rod holders on a 4×4, this problem no longer exists: Simply stand the rod up and work with both hands free.

You can now carry a complete live-bait system with you as well. This would include cast nets, a large bait tank, pumps, an aerator, and 5-gallon buckets that allow you to capture and keep live baits with you. If a blitz occurs, you have the option of snagging baits, collecting them, and keeping them alive for use either immediately or later in the day. This will be especially advantageous on those days when the fish are finicky and want the real thing.

You can carry a large cooler either inside your vehicle or, preferably, mounted outside in the front or rear. Having food, cool drinks, and a place to carry home any fish slated for the dinner table is a big plus. A 4×4 will also provide you with immediate protection and shelter if the weather quickly takes a turn for the worse.

Make sure you are fully aware of safety procedures, and carry the required safety and towing equipment in your vehicle at all times when on the sand. Always air down your tires so your 4×4 rides on top of the sand rather than sinking into it. Deflating your tires will increase their surface area, thereby reducing the pressure that the tires will exert on the sand. It's the basic snowshoe principle: pressure = force ÷ area of application. Before you go onto the sand, check with your local municipality for all regulations and required permit fees.

III

Fishing the Back Bays

6

Structure and How to Fish It

Back bays offer a wide variety of structures that can effectively be fished by the wading angler or by boat. Flats, sedges, holes, drop-offs, fingers, rip lines, bridges, docks, and bulkheads are all available. Identifying these structures and reading how water patterns set up around them will help you understand how fish will be factor into the equation. Using what you know about baits and their movements will also tell you how to fish a particular area. The biggest part of sportfishing from a professional guide's point of view is spotting an opportunity and effectively putting an offering in the place where we expect a predatory fish to be.

FLATS

Flats are truly beautiful, quiet, and serene environments that will vary in size and depth. Not all flats are the same. Some are covered completely by eelgrass, while others offer only patches of vegetation or are completely sand covered. Deep water can also be present in the flats areas and will appear as fingers or holes.

The topography of the flats is created by winter wind and storms that stir up the bay. Wind-generated waves, strong current flows, and increased tidal pushes all have an effect. These forces all push sand and reshape the bottom.

Deep-water depressions can also be created by these forces and make a flat more diverse and attractive to bait and gamefish. These depressions become highways for predators moving from area to area searching for food. Gamefish can also use them as escape routes when they themselves become the prey.

Fish feeding on the flats are on the hunt and less likely to be holding in a specific location. If fish are on top, you may see them tailing or witness submarinelike pushes of water from cruising fish. In the case of early-spring bluefish invasions, you could witness a blitz.

Working a Flat

Flats fishing is a specialty type of fishing. Tackle and methods are easily adapted to be productive in this skinny-water environment. You can access these areas by foot, and you'll often find that you have a whole flat—extending for miles—all to yourself.

Fishing a flat is an exploratory process. As you walk across, try to be as stealthy as possible. Your approach when entering should be slow and investigative: Fish may be right in front of you.

Fish will feed on a flat for different reasons; the angle of sunlight, wind direction, and weather are all important factors, as is the tide. Understanding tides will help you predict the changes that will occur during your fishing trip.

A good pair of polarized sunglasses, such as these Spotter Shades, is necessary when working sand flats to see the contrast between deep and shallow water. Freda

In this zone an angler using flies can have a real advantage. Because sound travels more quickly through water than through air, a fly will have less impact when it hits the water than would a jig or plug.

You should employ a steady, slow retrieve in this zone. If feeding fish are present and within reach, try to cast beyond them to their side and allow your offering to come past them. This will usually draw an aggressive strike. Still, there are times when fish are not feeding and will follow your fly or lure just out of curiosity. Try a twitch to imitate an injured prey that suddenly tries to escape the predator. Many times this will cause an instinctive strike whether the fish is hungry or not.

If you are serious about flats fishing, you will need a pair of quality polarized sunglasses with 100 percent blocking of ultraviolet light. Your glasses should reduce glare and allow you to see below the surface into the water. They should also reveal bottom contrasts due to different water depths. We recommend the Australian-made Spotters Sunglasses with VCE, Visual Contrast/Color Enhancement. You can check them out on the Web at www.spotters-shades.com. We have worn many polarized sunglasses while out on the water, and Spotters outperform them all. They are well worth the investment.

SEDGES

The sedge banks you'll find in many back bays are a nursery for all types of marine life. Sedges are composed primarily of mud with both decaying and fresh-growing vegetation. In our guiding area, the Sedge Islands in Barnegat Bay offer myriad water conditions, from shallow to deep, and from still to swift.

Because of deeper water sometimes associated with sedge areas, bait can abound in this zone for many months of the year. Bay anchovies, mullet, herring, killies, and silversides can readily be found in these nutrient-rich areas. As a result, the predators will be there, too.

Of particular interest along sedge banks are the rip lines that can form around points of land as they protrude into the bay. Strong tidal flows will flood these areas, particularly during new- and full-moon phases. The resulting strong currents will undercut the sedge banks, making deep channels that run right next to the bank.

Such steep drop-offs are ideal channels for predators to pin bait to the bank. If you're on shore, you will want to move away from the bank and cast to this region from there. Many times bass will be directly underneath any overhanging sedge grasses or in tight against the bank as they lie in wait for baitfish to be swept by at the mercy of the current.

Bank drop-offs are ideally fished from a boat: Drift down the center of the channel along the bank and cast to the shoreline. If one particular location along the bank constantly produces fish, anchor in the channel and drift your offering downcurrent to waiting fish.

At other times blind casting off the sedges where quick drop-offs occur is also very productive. Since the water is deep, fish will be out of sight. If baitfish are around, though, these areas are worth a cast.

BRIDGES

Many back bays in the Northeast abound with bridges. These structures are ideal locations for locating stripers, weakfish, and sometimes bluefish as they use the currents to their advantages.

In fact, many stripers will take up residence around bridge abutments all season long, including winter months. They expend less energy suspended in the eddies that form on the downcurrent side of these structures, allowing them to winter over in a lethargic state or wait for an abundance of food to be swept by.

The direction of the tide is the key to determining what side of the bridge will be more productive. Stripers can take up feeding positions on either side of the bridge and will usually face the current. The incoming-water side, called the front, may hold some fish positioned to attack bait before they get to the structure. The downcurrent side, or back, may hold bass that feed on the separated leftover bait. As front and back sides change with the flow of the tide, fish reposition themselves accordingly.

> **Tip**
> When fishing under bridge lights, make sure that you don't cast a shadow on the water. This unnatural moving shadow will scare predators.

Bridge supports vary from concrete pilings and steel beams to wooden pilings. Also associated with bridges are seawalls, piling clusters, rocks, and icebreakers. These solid artificial structures create eddies in the current—spots where the water is slower, or a depression in the current takes place. Technically your offering should be placed in the eddy because baitfish are helplessly swept past these locations.

Bridges offer artificial light that seems to collect baitfish in abundance. Fish that are feeding in front of the bridge usually work the dark side of its shadow line, while those feeding on the back side will hang in the light snatching bait emerging from the darkness. Baitfish will be blinded for a second as their pupils adjust to the new surroundings. That moment of disarray is an opportunity for a predator to act.

When gamefish are feeding on the surface, they are commonly found on the upcurrent (incoming) side of the bridge. Bass are instinctual predators but also learn when and where to hunt. The older they get, the smarter they get in terms of where to find food and how to better ambush it.

Baitfish are relatively no match for a predator waiting to attack. Bass, for instance, will stage in certain areas like the fronts of bridges, where they are positioned as a blockade for the small-sized baitfish. It seems they begin the attack before the bait can get to the safety of the bridge pilings.

One of the favorite ambush points for stripers is just behind the shadow line, out of sight. From this vantage point, baitfish will be silhouetted against the background. If you can, study fish-holding positions along the bridge when the water is clear and lights are at their brightest. This knowledge will aid you when the water is off color and illumination is weak.

Bridge Tackle, Working the Bridge, and Taming Big Fish

Big fish pull hard! It is absolutely necessary to overpower a bass in swift current. If a huge fish gets the chance, it will go right into structure and break you off. As far as bridge tackle is concerned, conventional gear is preferred over spinning. The advantages are better line control, lure presentation, and fish-fighting ability.

Stripers have huge fins and will use everything they have to prevent being pulled away from their structure. Remember, they are fighting for their lives and you are not. When hooked, most will dive deep and try to cut your line on any underwater obstruction that they can find. For this reason, we recommend spooling your reels with nothing less than 60- to 80-pound Stren Super Braid.

In the old days, bucktail jigs and plugs were the traditional weapons for bridge anglers. Today, however, the weighted soft shad bodies outperform all other artificial offerings. They work well at every water depth level.

Standard plugging techniques using the old standbys will work along most bridges; long casts usually are not necessary. Making an accurate cast is most important. The retrieve and the lure's action are also critical. The objective is simple with artificials: Make the lure resemble the local bait.

In most instances you will need to experiment to find the depth where fish are holding. Start by working the bottom. Cast your jig and let it settle to the bottom, then—with your rod parallel to the water—make short sweeps upward. This will hop the jig off the bottom as if it's injured and put it in front of the fish. The motion will attract the attention of any predatory fish.

Most strikes will happen when the jig is on the fall. You need to be alert and react fast. When a striper or other fish realizes that it has inhaled a foreign object, it will spit out the lure. With soft bait jigs, the strike is unmistakable. A prompt upward stroke with the rod is important in setting the hook and turning the head of a big bass.

> **Tip**
> If you can see feeding fish, try to cast beyond them and work toward them. Casting too close will spook them.

When using conventional tackle, make an underhand cast. Keep the rod parallel to the water and pointed at the target. Just before the jig is going to hit the water, thumb the spool, slowing the descent so that it makes a light landing and minimal splash. Be gentle. Reel slowly enough to maintain a tight connection to the jig as it swims past the structure. This will ensure that it maintains a uniform depth.

Every bridge has unique characteristics, including light and shadows, eddy patterns, and tidal flow speed. As with all types of fishing, bridge anglers must adapt by working all the different feeding zones. Vary your artificial selection and the lure speed until you find what is producing strikes.

Bridges at Night

Bridge fishing is generally more productive at night. Bass have amazing eyesight, and at night they have an advantage when bait passes through from the lighted area to the dark area, or vice versa. Also, bass have an extremely sensitive lateral line, which they use to detect the slightest movement as bait sweeps past. And they're equipped with a keen sense of smell. These senses combine to make the perfect predator. At night stripers shift their senses into high gear, and the slightest abnormal sound will put them on notice of your presence. Therefore, be quiet! Your skill with stealth will help you outsmart the fish.

BULKHEADS

Bulkheads are often employed along back bay inlets, where they shore up the surrounding banks. Without bulkheads in these locations, the strong tidal flows that increase in velocity due to a narrowing of the waterway leading to an inlet would constantly erode away at the bank. The bulkhead prevents this from happening. For the same reason, many bulkheads are located wherever a creek or river enters a back bay.

Bulkheads are awesome platforms for the fly, spin, or conventional angler. Because strong currents run along their sides, most will have deep water directly in front of them. If you're extremely careful, you can stand on the bulkhead and fish from it. You will need excellent balance, and it's crucial to always know where your feet are. If you can fish by standing behind the bulkhead and casting over it, we recommend that approach.

When fishing bulkheads when the current is moving, remember that holding fish sit with their noses into the current; your offering must also be facing into the current to appear real. You generally won't get a take on an improperly placed artificial bait. Your offering

Bulkheads that are paralleled by deep channels are ideal summer locations for trophy weakfish. Freda

should be downcurrent by the time it enters the strike zone. Good technique will help you score with regularity.

Bulkheads can be a fly fisher's dream because they offer deep water right at your feet. We recommend fast-sinking lines to get into the strike zone; 300- to 400-grain lines with small diameters descend quickly. We also like to use weighted flies like Bob Popovics's Jiggy, Bob Clouser's Clouser Minnows, and Lefty Kreh's Half-and-Halfs.

7

Springtime Success

Springtime along the Northeast Coast is a special time for every serious angler we know. Most of us have spent the winter months indoors, with the bulk of our fishing opportunities consisting of attending shows, seminars, and flea markets. Some more fortunate may have visited one of our southern meccas, where warm sunshine and bent rods filled each day.

But now Mother Nature levels the playing field for all of us. Increased amounts of sunlight, warmer air and water temperatures, and the return of migrating bait and fish have revitalized our enthusiasm for going fishing. The cure for cabin fever has finally arrived. The watching, listening, and practicing are over; it's now time to play the game once again.

But you just can't head in any direction or to any location to be successful in spring. If you are heading to the oceanside, you are heading in the wrong direction—particularly if it's March or early April. Instead, you should be heading to the backwaters: back bays, estuaries, tidal rivers, creek mouths, and flats.

WHY WE JUMP TO THE BACK

One of the keys to your early-season success is going to be finding the warmest water that you can. At the start of the season, water temperatures govern the migration patterns of striped bass, bluefish, and weakfish as they move from south to north along the Atlantic coast. Water temperatures also govern the movement of migrating bait back to any specific location and dictate the reappearance of many mud-dwelling invertebrates that had dug themselves in for the long winter.

Back bay waters produce the best results in spring because they warm up more quickly than the oceanside. Several factors contribute to this warming, but first let's look at the physical nature of water so we know what we're up against.

From a physical standpoint, water has a high heat capacity, which means it does not change temperature very quickly. In actuality, it takes 1 calorie of energy to raise 1 gram of water 1 degree Celsius. From a fisherman's standpoint, this means that water will warm up or cool down much more slowly than land.

For example, we have all experienced days during the early summer when air temperatures climb into the upper 80s or 90s. In the course of the day, the surfaces of asphalt streets become very hot; you cannot walk across them in your bare feet. A jump in the ocean, however, reveals a much colder temperature. We see the same phenomenon in late fall, when air temperatures can drop below freezing but ocean temperatures remain in the low 60s.

So we are at a disadvantage when spring fishing simply because of the physical nature of water. Back bays that were iced up for a good part of the winter can feature water temperatures in the upper 30s or low 40s when March finally arrives.

With each passing spring day, however, the angle of the sun increases in the sky, resulting in an increased amount of solar radiation reaching every square foot of earth in our hemisphere. This solar radiation is absorbed by both ocean and back bay waters. Warming commences.

Since back bays are shallower, they will warm more quickly than the deeper waters of the ocean. Along the eastern seaboard, we will see our western bayshores warming up most quickly since they will receive full exposure to the sun all day long. Contributing also to increased

Tip

For the warmest water temperatures, look to fish the outgoing tide at the end of a day. By this time the sun's rays will have warmed the water; temperatures can rise as much as 5 or 6 degrees. Combine this effect with warm-water runoff and it stimulates fish to feed. Incoming tides in early spring will bring in much colder ocean water and turn the bite off.

warming is that many back bay areas have dark mud bottoms that absorb solar radiation better than light sandy bottoms.

Runoff from spring rains also factors in. In this case, water will warm as it is absorbed into the ground and subsequently enters our back bays through rivers, creeks, and streams. These areas will constantly push a warmer water flow to the bay. Many times the mouths where waterways enter a bay will be several degrees warmer than the bay proper. For this reason, fishing around these areas can be very productive.

Keep in mind, however, that this scenario will not hold true if the ground is snow covered. If we have a late-winter snowstorm that deposits a significant amount of snow on the ground, or a cold early spring with a late thaw, all bets are off, because the runoff from the land will be cold.

In the early season, anywhere you can find water temperatures that break the 50-degree mark is a good place to start; warmer is even better. It's a good idea to carry a handheld thermometer with you if you're wading back bays. On a boat, use your temperature sensor.

Make mental notes of the water temperatures you find—or better yet, enter them into a logbook that you can reference at the start of each new season. This will give you a quick starting point and help cut down on your searching from year to year. The same conditions might very well be present.

Also look for warm-water discharges, particularly from power plants. Along the eastern seaboard, there are several locations in each state where such plants discharge warmer water, either through outflow pipes that lead directly into the bay or by means of creeks that carry the water to the bay. In either case, the warm water acts as a magnet for bait and gamefish. Often the water in these areas can be 10 to 15 degrees warmer. Many of these plants operate continuously throughout the year, so even in winter a significant temperature break can be noticed. Make a note where these areas are and fish them if regulations allow. In some locations these areas may be restricted for security reasons. If so, keep your distance and operate within the letter of the law.

EARLY-SEASON FISH BEHAVIOR

Let's turn our attention to the nature of the fish that we target in spring: striped bass, bluefish, and weakfish. With all three of these species returning in good numbers in spring, there will be many opportunities to catch good numbers of fish. There is, however, a short window of opportunity for catching the largest available fish of each species.

Our first target in the Northeast is the striped bass. As water temperatures warm, resident bass that have remained in our river systems and back bays throughout the winter will start to root through the mud for small worms and invertebrates. These first catches usually fall prey to anglers who are dead-sticking blood worms along the riverbanks or bayshores. These bass have been present locally all winter, but they only began to feed as the water warms.

> **Tip**
> If you are fly fishing for stripers in early spring, observe the anglers who are fishing blood worms in your area. If they are not catching fish, chances that you'll do so are slim. If blood worm anglers are having success, though, then at least you know that stripers are in the area and on the feed.

Three springtime events trigger the return of larger or adult bass into our waters: the herring run, the menhaden run, and the spawning urge of the striped bass. The exact timing of all three is ultimately dictated by rising water temperatures and will present a window of opportunity for trophy fish.

The spring herring run centers primarily on the alewife and blueback herring. Like the striped bass, these baits are anadromous—they seek out fresh water to spawn. In springtime they move from the ocean into freshwater rivers, creeks, tributaries, and ponds that have outflows to the ocean or back bay areas. These are big baits in the 6- to 12-inch range and will easily get the attention of large adult bass.

We usually see these two herring species in our home waters of New Jersey by the end of March, with the alewives making their appearance first. By the end of April, bluebacks dominate the run, which usually lasts through May. May is also be the best window of opportunity to hook into a trophy bass, because water temperatures will be approaching the 60-degree range.

At the same time these herring species are migrating into our backwaters, adult menhaden—commonly known as mossbunker or just bunker—are doing the same. These baitfish are one of the most important forage species found along the Atlantic seaboard. They, too, are members of the herring family, and have both recreational and commercial value.

Adult bunker will move up the coast in spring after they spawn off the mid-Atlantic states, entering the warmer backwaters to feed on phytoplankton and zooplankton. The phytoplankton are blooming in spring in response to increased amount of sunlight and the nutrient-rich runoff from surrounding fertilized lands. With an increase in the amount of phytoplankton, we quickly see a bloom of the microscopic zooplankton that feed on the phytoplankton. As a result, plenty of food is available for the bunker.

A proper livewell set-up is the key for maintaining healthy live bait. Oval and round styles are preferred. Caris

At the same time, striped bass have once again started to migrate from their winter grounds off the Carolinas northward along the coast. The adults are anadromous and on a mission to spawn. Therefore, they will seek out suitable freshwater locations to do so. As they make their way inshore to these freshwater locations, they will run right smack into the bunker.

Driven by their spawning urge, the males will usually arrive first, followed by the large females and finally the smaller females. These fish will start to enter freshwater tributaries when the water temperature reaches 49 degrees. Spawning will occur when temperatures increase to 58 to 64 degrees. Some trophy bass can be found at these times, with the largest females in the 30-, 40-, and even 50-pound ranges. The males will usually be in the teens and 20s.

With all the adult bunker present, these big bass have plenty to feed on, particularly when they come off their spawn. As long as the bunker are there, the bass will hold. During the 2003 spring season, our guiding area in Monmouth County, New Jersey, saw one of the most incredible runs of bunker and big bass that anyone alive today can recall. Bass in the 30-pound range became common catches for any angler, with or without experience. The number of 40-pound bass that were caught topped the century mark; six bass of more than 50 pounds were weighed in at local tackle shops. This run of bunker and bass lasted from mid-May through early July.

A window of opportunity also presents itself for big bluefish in springtime. Traditionally, bluefish move northward along the Atlantic seaboard on the heels of the passing mackerel run, picking away at these baits. This is an offshore event for the most part, but can occur within 5 miles of the beach depending on where the schools actually move through. Like other migrations, this is highly temperature sensitive.

When the big blues invade an area, it's time to take notice because they are in the 8- to 12-pound range. These blues are fast, mean, and green and are commonly referred to as "racers." They have disproportionately large heads compared to their long, lean bodies. Upon arrival, these blues will head for the warmest waters of the back bays with one thing in mind: food.

The window of opportunity for big blues lasts only about three weeks. After gorging themselves, these big brutes will quickly exit the bay and head out to the deeper offshore waters. Unlike the bass, blues don't spawn until summer, and then it's an open-ocean event.

In New Jersey, the big blues usually appear in back bays during the first several weeks of May. Farther south along the coast this occurs earlier; farther north, big blues arrive slightly later. One of the favorite locations to find Mr. Razor Lips is going to be up on the flats. It is not uncommon during this time period to find big blues racing through

Tip

When wading out to a sandbar in a back bay, a thorough knowledge of how the tides affect the height of the water in a given location is extremely important. You don't want to get stranded on the bar as the water fills in behind you.

these areas like underwater submarines, torpedoing anything that comes into their range.

The presence of big weakfish will also coincide and overlap with the presence of stripers and bluefish, thereby providing a true smorgasbord of big-fish opportunities. The big weakfish that enter our back bay waters in spring are spawners, just like many of our striped bass. These big fish are commonly called tiderunners because their movements are associated with the changing tides.

Grass shrimp are another key springtime bait that serves as forage for stripers, blues, and weakfish. Freda

These spawners are searching out suitable structure in close proximity to submerged eelgrass beds to spawn. Weakfish are not anadromous and will stay in the brackish waters of bays and estuaries rather than seeking out freshwater areas. In fact, a heavy freshwater runoff from spring storms can quickly lower the salinity of a bay, sending these fish looking for a more suitable saline environment.

Spring weakfish will range in size from 3 to 11 pounds, but it should come as no surprise if bigger fish are taken. Several years ago, a spawning-season weakfish of 18 pounds was caught. This fish was taken in the Sandy Hook area.

In New Jersey, the window of opportunity for big weakies is from the first or second week in May until the middle of June. In other locales along the Atlantic Coast, this time frame will vary somewhat as the fish move from south to north along the coast. When their spawn is over, big weakfish will not remain in the bay for summer but rather head back to the ocean. A few stragglers, however, can still be caught.

With a good percentage of our trophy spring fish consisting of spawning bass and weakfish, it is critical that you practice catch and release if the fish are not spawned out. These fish should be given a chance to drop their eggs before they are taken to the dinner table. In doing so, you will be doing your part to help to ensure that our fishery continues in earnest for many years to come. Having a trophy shot at all three species in any given day is quite an exciting way to start off a new season.

Inshore and Offshore Boat Fishing

8

Going to Sea: Boat Mechanics

While fishing from land-based structures offers a rewarding placidity, there are many times when the versatility of a boat will simply put more fish on your line. Today boat manufacturers are making it more and more affordable for saltwater anglers to turn the key and enjoy a hassle-free experience on both inshore and offshore waters. Years ago, it was unheard of for larger center consoles to be making canyon runs in search of offshore species. Today it's a regular occurrence to see these deep-V'd "speed rockets" running to the bluewaters in search of pelagic species.

Most northeastern boat fishers, however, will spend their time along the inshore waters and back bays fishing for striped bass, bluefish, weakfish, and other inshore gamefish. Whether it be fly fishing, plugging, jigging, trolling, wreck fishing, or big-game hunting on the offshore grounds, one factor needs to be on the top of every boater's list: safety.

SAFETY

Going to sea is a serious game that many new boaters take for granted. Like driving an automobile on public roads and highways, however, boating features certain "rules of the road." It is extremely important that boaters fully understand the ocean's unpredictable behavior, and we urge all anglers to take a Coast Guard–approved boating safety class before they head to sea.

Smart boaters treat their rigs the way good athletes treat their bodies, always ensuring that it's running in tip-top condition. Boat

> **Tip**
> Keep a safety checklist on board at all times and perform regular quick examinations of all working parts on board, including horn, oil level, fuel level, and electronic functions. Do a lifesaving and first-aid equipment check as well to ensure that life jackets, flares, EPIRB, fire extinguishers, throw buoys, first-aid gear, and other pertinent materials are all on board and in working order.

failure at sea is not a pleasant experience, especially if you're not prepared with the proper towing insurance, safety equipment, and electronics to reach help quickly. Always make it a point to go over the workings of your boat with your fellow anglers. If you're fishing alone, leave word with a close friend or relative as to where you plan to fish that day.

Never leave the dock without the proper safety equipment required by the Coast Guard. Type 1 life jackets, flares, a fire extinguisher, a portable horn, a whistle, a compass, a throw buoy, an oar, extra lines, and a first-aid kit are all standard pieces of equipment that should always be on your vessel. It's wise to carry a cell phone should your radio go down, along with handheld GPS and VHF (as backups to your standard electronics), extra food, beverages, matches, additional clothing, and foul-weather gear. If you fish offshore (20 nautical miles and farther), a life raft, offshore survival suits, and Class 1 EPIRB (emergency position-indicating radio beacon) should always be on your boat and in perfect working order.

EPIRBs are to offshore fisherman what avalanche beacons are to backcountry climbers and skiers. Should your vessel go down, an EPIRB will send an immediate signal to the Coast Guard with your exact position. Many experienced offshore fishermen have a single EPIRB mounted on their vessel and keep others stored away with the survival gear.

FISHABILITY: BOAT LAYOUTS

Now that you're equipped to hit the water safely, what boat will you choose to go fishing in? There are many different makes, models, and manufacturers to choose from, and deciding on the type of fishing you like to do should dictate the type of layout and hull you choose.

Hulls

Hull designs can be divided into three major categories: deep-V, modi-fied-V, and flat-bottomed boats. As with the majority of boat-purchasing decisions, finding the right hull for your particular style of fishing usu-ally comes down to a compromise. Take the basic inshore northeastern fisherman, for instance. This angler likes to run all-out in heavy seas during the summer months and fall migrations, and he fishes in open-water situations where ocean swells roll and heavy chop is a regular occurrence. Deep V, right? Not necessarily. In addition, this angler also likes to do a significant amount of drift fishing, fly fishing, and shallow-water exploring during spring in and along the backwaters. Surely he should be looking for a flat-bottomed boat, right? In a case like this, the angler usually takes the middle road and goes with a modified-V hull that offers stability while drift fishing, stealth for the shallows, enough hull V to comfortably ride the seas, and greater freeboard that will ensure safety out on the open swells.

Very few boat manufacturers make this type of vessel better than Parker Boats out of Beaufort, North Carolina. There is no mass-pro-duction mentality at Parker Boats, whose products are known for being overbuilt and underpriced. Since the late 1960s, Linwood Parker has been building fishing boats for anglers who seek maximum value without spending a fortune. These boats feature wide flared bows and classic lines that provide stability, fishability, and seaworthiness. Most notable is Parker's line of 18- to 28-foot center consoles and sport

Captain Jim Freda's 21 Parker Sport Cabin provides a dry, stable ride in all seasons with a lot of fishing room besides. Quigley

cabins that are built on Special Edition and XL Modified V hulls. These boats offer the best of both worlds: a smooth and solid feel when running through the rough stuff, and stealth and stability when fishing the back bays and shallows.

Layout

So you've chosen your hull; now what about a layout? Offshore fishermen still prefer the comfort and reliability that an inboard diesel sportfisher offers. Inshore, hard-core purists and saltwater fly fishers still prefer center consoles. They offer maximum fishability by allowing you to fish from all aspects of the boat comfortably, and with a small amount of modification can still keep you out of the elements by adding T-tops and isinglass curtains. Sport cabins and walkaround cuddies add another dimension in that they provide more shelter, storage, and sleeping configurations than a traditional center console. Whatever the case may be, make sure that you choose a hull style and deck layout that fits your style of fishing.

ELECTRONICS

Today's technology allows fishers to exactly pinpoint wrecks, ridges, holes, offshore canyons, and other structures. In fact, the technology has become so advanced that most electronics manufacturers are producing three-dimensional color fishfinders, global positioning ystem (GPS) units, and chart plotters that offer incredible detail. Using electronics to your advantage is an art form. In addition to finding fish, electronics serve as safety devices, helping anglers navigate and communicate on the water. During the days of old, only the larger, offshore sportfishing boats mounted a panel of sophisticated electronics. Today pretty much all of your midsized 20- to 30-foot fishing machines sport a quiver of technology.

Until the early 1990s, most fishing vessels used loran (long-range navigational systems) to get from point A to point B out on the high seas. Loran units navigate through radio transmissions, sending to the loran transceiver numbers and displays that represent the time difference between two radio signals. These time differences, or TDs, are represented by lines of positions on your coastal navigational charts. Besides telling you where you are between positions, loran also plots a course from point to point, offers speed calculations, and gives you your estimated time of arrival along with the distance you still have to reach your destination.

> **Tip**
>
> When searching for fish out on the open water, use your radar to locate tightly packed working birds or fishing fleets that are out of sight. By setting your radar to the harbor or sensitive setting, you will be able to pick up groups of tightly packed "specks" on your screen. In many cases, these are birds hovering over schools of feeding fish on the surface. When searching for fishing fleets, set your unit on the sea or midsensitivity settings to locate boats that are bunched together on the screen. Once located, you can obtain distance and heading right from the radar and plot them into your GPS.

Although many boaters still use their loran units for navigation, most have switched over to the more user-friendly GPS units. In addition to offering ease of use, these units do everything a loran can and then some. From chart navigation to creating routes, identifying depths and tides, and marking obstacles, these highly refined electronic units make it very difficult for anglers to lose their way on the water.

What most boaters do not realize about GPS is that it is useless in the fog unless you have a radar unit on board to warn other boats that are navigating the same waters. Sure, knowing how to use GPS effectively will get you home in the fog—but what about the inherent dangers other vessels possess? Two boats navigating the same waterway in the fog without radar can lead to serious injury to both your rig and your crew, and in most instances these injuries are fatal. More and more small boats are installing radar units for this very reason, and if you plan to buy a boat for any type of serious saltwater fishing, we recommend that you purchase one.

From loran units to radar, GPS, and color sounders, small boats now have the same fishfinding advantages as their larger offshore counterparts. From a purely safety standpoint, every fishing vessel that ventures out into the salt water should be equipped with at least the bare minimum of electronics: handheld VHF radio, GPS, and a depth sounder/fishfinder. The more serious you get about fishing, and the farther you venture offshore, the more advanced your electronics should get. These "must-have" tools allow you to navigate unfamiliar waters both in daylight and darkness, and—more importantly—allow you to call for help should you experience difficulties.

Let's assume that you're having a tremendous afternoon on the water. The fish are biting, and you and your crew decide to stay on the bite right through dark. On the way home it's pitch black, and you have many narrow channels and shallow sandbars to navigate in order to find your port. A standard GPS and chart plotter will show you within a few feet where your vessel is at all times and accurately draw you a map to follow for safe navigation back to port.

Or suppose you decide to fish an inshore wreck 7 to 8 miles off-shore. You are the only boat there, and after a great day of fishing you turn the key and your tried-and-trusted new engine won't kick over. Picking up your VHF radio and calling Sea Tow or the Coast Guard will let you sleep in your own bed that night rather than spending it out at the wreck waiting for someone to come by. Catch our drift? By having even the basic no-frills electronics on board, you greatly reduce the chance of getting into serious trouble on the water.

Many times, using your electronics to find fish will make the difference between a full and an empty box as well. Today's GPS units allow you to store multiple waypoints that precisely pinpoint the wrecks, ridges, sandbars, reefs, and depths you plan to fish. While GPS stores favorable fishing locations, fishfinders allow you to pick up real-time readings of bottom structures, schooling fish, and baits by sending signals through the transducer. These signals bounce off the bottom, pick up the reading, then echo back to the transducer and put the mark on the sonar screen. These sonar units also give you sea-surface temperatures identifying temperature changes and warm-core eddies that are likely to hold fish.

STORAGE

One of the issues that anglers struggle with on smaller boats is tackle and gear storage. Countless days are spent out at sea in search of more than one type of fish or fishing situation. On any given day, boaters can

> **Tip**
> With the new soft bait revolution, try using the soft tackle bags by Shimano. These allow you to store many different sizes and colors of soft baits in one unit that can fit easily in just about any storage compartment.

T-tops and aftermarket rod rocket launchers like this multiple custom fly rod holder from Bluewater Designs, Bristol, CT, are available from many of the independent T-top manufacturers. Quigley

spend the morning fly fishing the backwaters, anchor up on a wreck and bottom fish in the late morning, then troll their way inshore for small tuna and dolphin. Here is where the storage issue comes into play.

Simply put, most boat manufacturers do not offer adequate rod storage right off the factory floor, forcing anglers to get creative by adding aftermarket rocket launchers and under-gunnel rod mounts. Properly placed on your vessel, anglers can store upward of 20 rods on any given day. Blue Water Designs of Bristol, Connecticut (www.blue-waternet.com), makes a wide range of fly-rod holders, including a model that will fit into your existing rocket launchers. This allows you to convert from spinning- to fly-rod storage easily.

Terminal tackle, lures, flies, hooks, and jigs should all be stowed inside, away from the raw salt air. Many anglers now use different sizes of Plano boxes to make custom tackle lockers in order to keep gear secure and organized. Ameripack's (www.ameripack.com) new series of fly boxes give anglers the ability to store a maximum amount of flies in one box. The company also carries a complete line of waterproof boxes for cameras and tackle.

Professional captains stay organized when it comes to tackle and gear because they know that clutter means confusion. When the action starts, you want your gear out of the way, yet easily accessible.

9

Spring and Summer Boat Tactics

Finding fish in and along the coastal backwater system by boat begins with a basic understanding of spring migrations. Many factors come into play when trying to locate migratory species, and in this chapter we will discuss our tactical approach to finding fish from a boat along inshore back bays and tidal rivers.

Structure, bait, water temperature, and migration paths are all important factors to consider when searching back bays and tidal rivers. Whether it be spring or summer, these factors tell you where to start. Once you find the fish, of course, getting them to eat is another story, and an alignment of all of the above "stars" will not necessarily put fish on the end of the line.

Back bays and tidal rivers present tremendous opportunity for finding northeastern gamefish such as striped bass, bluefish, and weakfish during spring and summer months. At this time, fish migrate up the coast in search of baitfish. These inner coastal waters are natural spawning areas for local forage. When tides ebb and flow through these backwaters, water temperatures and bait movements fluctuate with currents and in many cases dictate feeding patterns through the inland tidal water system. In our local waters, one of the best places to intercept this feeding is in and around the currents that move by structure.

FISHING BACK BAY STRUCTURE

Fishing structure from a boat can be much more difficult than on foot. With your feet planted firmly on the ground, presenting a plug, fly, or

Captain Gene Quigley's 23 foot Parker SE is the perfect boat for all of your inshore and midshore saltwater fishing. Quigley

jig in moving currents is a simple matter: Just cast upcurrent and allow your lure to swing through, using your judgment by fishing different depths in order to find where the fish are holding.

From the boat, however, there are many more factors to take into consideration. If you allow your boat to move with the current, many times your presentation will not offer that ever-so-deadly "swing" through the current path. If you're fishing a fast-moving current or rip, more often than not the boat's drift puts you out of position before you can really work the area effectively. Stealth and boat noise also come into play: Fish will spook easily when confronted by the noise of an engine or hull slap on a boat. There are two ways to overcome this latter problem. First, stem the current with the engine or, better yet, trolling motors, to allow your line to swing through the current as a land-based angler would. Or, if boat noise is an issue and you know the fish are holding, anchor up away from where the fish are and cast into the zone to allow for the natural swing.

Still, there are more times than not when having a boat in the backwaters will give you an advantage over anglers afoot. Structures such as channel drop-offs and flats are often simply not accessible by foot. These areas, too, may require a stealthy approach, especially along the endless flats where water is often extremely shallow. Many anglers today have borrowed from our southern counterparts by adopting sight-fishing tactics with fly and light spinning tackle. Here boat anglers use smaller 14- to 17-foot flats skiffs and pole the shallows from a platform looking for fish. This is a highly effective way of locating striped bass up in the shallows, and has become extremely popular with fly and light-tackle guides from Maryland to Maine. For the average angler, however, purchasing a flats skiff for all of your northeast inshore saltwater fishing would not be a wise choice, seeing as much of the season is spent along the outer beaches in the more temperamental ocean waters.

One technique that works well for anglers who don't have flats skiffs, but do have hulls with drafts shallow enough to drift in 2 feet of water, is to come above the flat and drift through with your engine off. Different from the traditional sight-and-stalk approach, this approach uses blind-casting techniques that let you cover a lot of water by fanning casts around all 360 degrees of the boat. Pay particular attention to any movement on the water's surface, as subtle as it may be. The slightest ripple or swirl could indicate feeding, and a quick cast in that direction will usually lead to a strike.

We always try topwater poppers in the shallows first in order to entice wary stripers and bluefish to crash the bait on the surface. When spin fishing, we utilize smaller 1-ounce poppers like the Gibbs Polaris or the Stillwater Smack It. The Smack It in particular seems to produce more strikes on the flats than do heavier sinking poppers made from wood. Because these lures are made of plastic, they will float on the surface. This allows you to work the plug fast and furious, but also slow and lethargic.

Channel edges and drop-offs also present tremendous opportunities for backwater boat anglers. In our home waters of Barnegat Bay, these locations are where we see the greatest success between April and July when targeting New Jersey's famed tiderunner weakfish. Every spring, large schools of 8- to 13-pound tiderunners enter our bays to spawn in and around the shallow eelgrass flats that lie in the center and eastern walls of our southern bays. The actual spawn generally takes place in the dark of night immediately after the last moon in May. During daylight, these fish set up deep in the main channels. As evening approaches, they will stage, and feed, along the edges of the shallow eelgrass flats, where the flat meets the deep channel. Working these channel edges with a fly, plug, or soft bait jig offers the best opportunity to catch these colorful fish before spawning occurs.

Anytime you're fishing a channel, wind direction and current flow will determine which side to fish. Winds and currents that come from the southern quadrant will push bait off the south edge of the flat into the channel. When winds and current blow out of the northern quadrant, look to the north edge of the channel. As small grass shrimp and spearing push off the grassy flats onto the channel, gamefish will hold just off the edge, ready to ambush the defenseless forage. If you're fishing the south edge of the channel, place the boat a cast away from the edge of the flat and work the entire slope—from the edge of the flats to the bottom of the channel—while the boat drifts naturally in a northern direction. In this situation, we achieve success by working the fly or jig slowly along the bottom with a slight twitching or jerking motion.

When trying to match small baits like grass shrimp or spearing, we have found that slender, 3- to 5-inch artificials work best. The staple for spin and conventional fishers here in New Jersey is the pink Fin-S fish on a ⅜- or ½-ounce lead jighead. We recommend using the banana-shaped Oldham "screw-in" jighead. The bait will stay on the jighead for many more fish because it's twisted onto the jig and held tightly to the hook by a corkscrew wire.

New to the soft bait scene are the Storm and Tsunami baits. These soft baits actually have the lead impregnated into the rubber and come in a great variety of new colors. These are the most realistic soft baits on the market today; in many cases they're outfishing other soft baits at a rate of three to one.

One of the most effective ways to fish coastal backwater systems is to fly fish. Saltwater fly fishing has become extremely popular during the last 10 years; it's our method of choice when targeting striped bass, bluefish, and weakfish during spring and summer months. Whether you need a surface, subsurface, or deep-water presentation, you can effec-

> **Tip**
> When fly fishing for weakfish and stripers with sinking lines, your leaders should be short, anywhere from 3 to 4 feet long. This allows the fly to sink at the same rate as the sinking fly line. When you use longer leaders with sinking lines, the fly line will sink faster than the fly, presenting an unnatural dragging appearance underwater.

tively achieve it today with a fly rod. When fishing these channel drops for stripers and weakfish with a fly, we use 300- to 400-grain sinking lines that sink at a rate of 6 to 8 inches per second along with weighted flies like the Popovics Jiggy or Clouser Minnow. These flies both have leadheads that give the presentation an up-and-down "jigging" motion much like an injured baitfish or darting grass shrimp. When done correctly, the fly can be even more deadly than soft baits or plugs because the takeback can be controlled and performed at any speed or frequency with a hand-over-hand retrieve. Whichever method you prefer, be sure to bring your offering right up to the boat before picking up for another cast. Many times wary weakfish or striped bass will follow your fly or jig right to the boat and hit at the last minute.

In addition to the famed spring weakfish run here in the mid-Atlantic backwaters, we see a significant northern migration of big spring bluefish that come into backwaters to feed. All of these channel edges and flats are prime areas to score with bluefish as well. Unlike the slow and lethargic presentations made for weakfish, bluefish prefer more of a strident, fast presentation. We definitely leave the soft baits in the boat when these big 'gators come around, and prefer to use more durable tackle such as metals, single-hook plugs, poppers, and epoxy flies. Probably the most effective way to locate bluefish in the backwa-

The Master, Bob Popovics, and Capt. Gene Quigley with a 12-pound Barnegat Bay tiderunner. Quigley

ters is with topwater poppers. In these calmer backwater systems, using floating plastic poppers (like the Stillwater mentioned above) allows you to control your retrieve without having to work so hard to keep the presentation afloat.

As the first blues enter the Atlantic backwater systems, they head up to the shallow, warmer mudflats. These are the generally the largest fish of the run, and can weigh anywhere from 8 to 12 pounds. Since water temperatures in these areas have a tendency to rise quickly with the spring sun, hordes of baitfish gather for warmth and protection. By casting topwater poppers up and around the flats, you can quickly discover where they're holding, and hungry bluefish are sure to be attracted to the constant commotion from up above. Generally speaking, we have a tendency to move the popper very quickly across the surface, almost with no pause or hesitation at all. Because bluefish are usually found in schools, this creates a competitive atmosphere for feeding blues, and will draw more fish closer to the boat for other anglers on board.

Bait-and-switch techniques are used widely by spin and fly fishers on both inshore and offshore grounds. Here we employ a two-angler team concept. The first angler spin-casts a hookless popper out as far as he can and works it back to the boat at a steady fast pace. As the fish begins to come up on the popper, the first angler speeds up the retrieve

Use a hookless Smack-It Popper and a Bob's Banger for the ultimate bait and switch technique on the fly. Quigley

in order to draw the blues into fly-casting range. Next, the second angler, armed with a 9- or 10-weight fly rod, will cast directly in front of the path of the hookless popper. As the two meet, the first angler rips the plug out of the water, and the fish are drawn to the fly for an instant hookup.

New Jersey fly-fishing legend Bob Popovics invented a topwater popper for fly fishermen called the Bob's Banger. The Banger has a large circular foam head that does not taper from one end to the other. This creates a hefty *plop-plop* sound that drives fish crazy. The Banger also tracks straight and will not roll like many of the boilermaker-style poppers on the market today. Originally designed for bluefish, the Banger's foam head can be easily changed to a larger or smaller size, or replaced when chewed up by 'gator blues. We like to fish the Banger with a hand-over-hand retrieve. This allows us to control the speed, pause, and momentum of the fly because one hand is always working the popper.

For most northeastern coastal anglers who fish from a boat, the striped bass is on the top of the fishing target list. Finding backwater stripers from boats in spring is a lot harder than finding them in fall along the outer beaches. In fall, many factors like dive-bombing seagulls and gannets tell us where stripers are pushing up bait. In spring, however, most of the visual clues are subtle at best. Usually, anglers depend on their knowledge of the area to find fish. For us, structure means everything, especially where it meets currents. The structure can be man-made, like bulkheads, islands, or jetties, or can be more natural— sandbars, drop-offs, rips, and deep-water holes. Spring stripers can be a funny bunch. Some days you will catch them on every cast. Go back the next day, same spot, same tide, have a different wind direction, and you won't get as much as a hit.

Early in the season, when water temperatures are cool (45 degrees to 50 degrees), cut baits like bunker, clams, herring, and mackerel (discussed in chapter 4) usually yield the best results. Fish them either at anchor or on the drift. Most boat anglers, however, will choose to anchor above or along structures and fish these baits on the bottom by using a three-way or a fishfinder rig. As water temps reach into the low and mid-50s, livelining techniques (discussed in chapter 14) will generally catch more fish, because stripers become somewhat aggressive and will begin to chase their prey. It isn't until water temperatures reach the mid- to high 50s that we start using artificials and flies from the boat.

BOAT POSITIONING IN THE BACKWATERS

Most of our boat fishing in the backwaters is done by drifting, or "stemming" currents while using light-tackle artificials or fly-fishing tactics. Finding the right position or drift for the boat in the backwaters is a challenge for many anglers. With limited space in many areas, obtaining the perfect drift or finding that "sweet spot" where fish are holding can mean all the difference in the world. When we approach a new area in the boat, we try to drift from every possible angle in order to cover the entire section before we declare it a "time to move" situation. Always take wind and current speed into account and position the boat at random spots above the underwater structure or above the lane you intend to drift. Allow the boat to drift through naturally, fishing in every possible direction.

With the right drift, the key to success lies with the presentation. We prefer to cast slightly in front of the boat's drift direction, and off at a 45-degree angle. This allows your presentation to naturally work its way back through the current and cover water in front, to the side, and behind you, ending in a natural swing. The faster the boat is moving, the wider the front-to-back radius cast you should make.

When you know fish are holding in a specific area—say, a sod bank or a tidal creek mouth—stemming the current by holding the boat in place while at throttle is a deadly method. This tactic requires two or more anglers to be aboard, one constantly at the wheel while the others fish. The boat handler will need to find the right throttle speed in order to keep the boat still in the current. When done right, the anglers should feel as if they are standing on solid ground, not moving at all. The key to obtaining this again lies with wind direction/speed, and current direction/speed. All boats drift and turn with current and wind differently, so there are no set rules as to where your initial start position needs to be. Start by pointing the bow of the boat against the direct position the current is running, then adjust the position of the bow to compensate for the wind direction. For example, if the current is running down from north to south, and the wind is coming from the east, the bow of the boat should lie somewhere between the north and east arms of the compass. Always turn your engine all the way into the wind. Stronger currents in this situation would dictate pointing the bow in a more north-northeast direction. Stronger winds than current, and the bow should point east-northeasterly. Utilize the same "front to back—45 degrees to the side" casting style that was discussed above when stemming currents while drift fishing.

THE SHRIMPIN' GAME

Earlier in this chapter, we discussed spring tactics for tiderunner weak-fish here in New Jersey. One technique that has been extremely successful for us has been something called shrimpin', which will work in any locale where bait is present. Used mainly for catching tiderunner weakfish in late-spring and early-summer months, chumming with live grass shrimp will attract many other species into your slick, including stripers, bluefish, and fluke. This technique has been a Barnegat Bay staple long since before we came on the scene, and for some of the old-timers here in southern New Jersey it is still the *only* way to fish.

We usually start to chum with grass shrimp for weakfish and stripers just after the weakfish spawn in late May. During many seasons, this can be the only way to put trophy postspawn tiderunner weakfish in the boat in late spring/early summer. The best part about it, however, is that it's a heck of a lot of fun.

To start, you need live shrimp. There are two kinds of shrimp in south Jersey waters, grass shrimp and sand shrimp. Sand shrimp are generally the first to show in great numbers in our bays during late-winter months. These shrimp are larger than the grass shrimp (about 1½ to 2 inches long) and have black spots running all along their tan bodies, giving them the nickname "salt and pepper" shrimp. The grass shrimp

Tip

When anchoring up for the shrimpin' game, use a double anchoring system instead of the traditional single anchor off the bow. Drop one anchor off the stern and then drive across or perpendicular to the current. Let out double the amount of line you normally would to hold bottom. Then drop the front anchor off the bow and reverse the boat back to the stern anchor while your mate or second angler pulls in the slack and secures the stern line. After the stern line is secured, pull down and secure the bow line. You can now use the entire side of the boat to fish, and the current runs starboard to port rather than bow to stern. This will also help you slow down the current: The boat now serves as a barrier, allowing the bait (shrimp) and your presentation to move back into the slick slowly, rather than being swept through high in the water column.

spawns in early spring, just after the sand shrimp, and is only ½ to 1 inch in length. Grass shrimp are very translucent, with a greenish tan tint. Both baits work equally well. Most local tackle shops here carry these live baits; the cost is usually around $6 to $8 a quart, depending on availability.

In order to start shrimpin', you will need a good system to keep the baits fresh and alive. Local anglers have devised a screened cooler and rack system that is foolproof and can keep 6 to 8 quarts of shrimp fresh and lively for an entire day. Picking the right location while shrimpin' is crucial to your success. As a general rule, outgoing tides will work best. It's during these tides that the back bay eelgrass flats, where these bait live, are flushed out with the ebbing tide. Try to position the boat along a grassy sod bank or off the edge of a flat or channel drop-off. This method of fishing will require your boat to be at anchor. Once secured, we like to spike the water heavily at first, throwing anywhere from 5 to 10 baits every 30 seconds or so. Once the first fish is caught, we will slow down the slick considerably and throw four to six shrimp every minute or so. This is done in order to keep the bite going for the entire tide and not overfeed the fish.

There are many ways to fish in the shrimp slick. With light conventional tackle, we will place one or two shrimp on a single hook with a float rig. We use a size 2 or 4 hook for this type of fishing. Set your float according to the depth as the bait is swept back into the current. Be sure to experiment if you don't receive any hits. If you're fishing water depths of, say, 12 to 14 feet, set the float 4 or 5 feet above the hooked bait and adjust deeper from there. With this technique, you will literally free-line the bait back into the slick with absolutely no tension at all. When the float goes down, set up on the fish quickly.

For spin fishers who prefer to use artificials, cast-and-retrieve methods can also be employed. Here you will use a ¼- to ½-ounce sparsely tied bucktail jig or dart. Attaching a live shrimp to the hook is optional. Cast the bucktail back into the slick and allow it to sink to the bottom. Then bring the jig in very slowly with an up-and-down jigging motion to give the appearance of a darting shrimp.

Probably the most effective way to fish the shrimp slick is with a fly rod. Bob Popovics's Ultra Shrimp is the most realistic imitation of a grass or sand shrimp that we've seen, and it has proven extremely deadly with the chumming technique. On many occasions, we've seen the Ultra Shrimp outfish live hooked baits four to one.

For this type of fly fishing, we use lighter 7- and 8-weight outfits. Depending on depth, you will want to use a fly line that can get you down to where the fish are feeding. In shallower waters (4 to 8 feet) where currents are slight, a weight-forward intermediate line is the best choice. In faster currents and deeper waters, 300- to 400-grain sinking lines are better. There are two techniques we use to fish the Ultra Shrimp. The first is to cast the fly out and let it sink, retrieving with a very slow and erratic movement. The second technique requires you to drift the fly back into the slick much like the real baits. Both work equally well, depending on the bite, and make no mistake about it, weakfish and stripers will hit your offering with a vengeance. So hold on tight!

10

Fall Boat Tactics

"**Y**ou should have been here yesterday! There were fish everywhere." Only the day you go out, there are no signs of life. You hear the constant chatter on the radio, and everyone is taking about where they had 'em yesterday.

There's an old saying about finding fish: "If you heard about it, forget about it." These are good words to go by. Chasing "ghosts" is never a good way to spend your day fishing.

So how do you find fish by boat out on the open seas? Some days it's simple: Find the birds and you've found the fish. These are the incredible fall days when striped bass, bluefish, bonito, and false albacore feed on the surface all day long and literally anything you cast in the mix will produce a strike. Unfortunately, these days are few and far between. On ordinary days, you need to go out and hunt for fish in the ocean.

BOAT HANDLING THE BLITZ

As tremendous as it can be, working blitzing fish under birds does have its challenges. With all the bait and commotion, many times these fish, particularly little tuna, become very selective; only the most calculated approach and presentation will work. No matter what the situation, there are many tactics that we employ and follow for success.

First, never, ever drive the boat directly into breaking fish. This will without a doubt put the fish down and limits your opportunities for a hookup. This presents a problem when working speedy blitzing false albacore and bonito—these fish have a tendency to move very fast and can be up on top for as little as a few seconds. Add a few boats into the equation chasing the same pods of fish and you've got a competition to see who can get the fish faster—definitely not a smart or safe way to go fishing. Try looking for feeding patterns before you play the chasing game. Many days these fish will set up in a specific area to feed on multiple pods of small baits, attacking in a repetitive pattern. Here you can anticipate the stop and be in the vicinity before the targets come up. Now your boat is in good position to be on top of the fish quickly.

> **Tip**
> When you see a large group of birds sitting on the water, stop upcurrent and take one drift using deep-water jigs or soft baits. Many times birds will hold in a tight group over a body of fish and/or bait that is deep in the water column. If you mark fish during the drift, be sure to set a waypoint on your GPS so you can pinpoint the holding grounds after the birds fly away.

Another successful technique is to get set upwind of the area and drift through. We use this technique more often when stripers and blues are working baits on the surface; these fish have a tendency to come up on one school of bait rather than chasing multiple schools, like the little tuna do.

No one tactic works all the time when fishing under birds, and we have had success using many different techniques when fishing the blitzes for multiple species. Meaning, the tactics and techniques proven to work on little tuna do not necessarily correspond to the techniques we use for striped bass or bluefish. Furthermore, the same tactics and techniques do not necessarily work the same today as they did under similar conditions on past days. It's important to employ many different approaches when one doesn't produce.

LITTLE TUNA: INSHORE STRATEGIES FROM THE BOAT

During early fall (September and October), most of our boat fishing revolves around chasing false albacore and Atlantic bonito with fly and light spinning tackle. We have seen many anglers get downright furious when targeting these fish simply because they do not know the techniques for success. As we mentioned earlier in this chapter, these little

Hard-fighting false albacore like this speedster caught by Gary Heger are readily available from September through October from North Carolina to Massachusetts. Quigley

tuna can move faster than a cheetah at times, cruising from one pod of bait to another and attacking in a rank-and-file military fashion. Boat positioning and quick, accurate casts are the most important factors for scoring with little tuna. Try to look for a feeding pattern. Many days we have witnessed large schools of false albacore working four to six pods of bay anchovies all in a 200-yard radius. Look for the pattern so you can set up and have your boat in the vicinity before the action happens.

When fishing with a partner, always alternate by having one dedicated angler and one dedicated skipper behind the helm. Guides will always catch more little tuna than the average fisherman simply because they are always on the throttle and put their anglers in position quickly while the school is still up. Once the boat reaches the school, the boat needs to stop and stay stationary. Just cutting the throttle won't cut it. We all know that boats don't have brakes, and a good captain will put the boat in reverse at the right moment to stop on a dime. This allows the angler to cast and begin retrieving immediately, without having to recapture any slack in the line from the boat moving in the direction of the cast. Remember, most takes while fishing for little tuna come within the first few cranks of the reel or strips of the fly line—assuming you have positioned your fly or lure in the midst of the breaking fish.

> ### Tip
> When approaching schools of breaking fish from the boat, never point the bow directly into the action. This will push the boat into the breaking fish after you have put it in neutral. Rather, always try to come in from a side angle from upwind. This will position your boat directly parallel to the breaking fish and allow all the anglers on your boat to get into the action.

Always try to be as accurate as you can by getting your offering into the action while the fish are still up. If the fish are up, they're still feeding, and your fly or lure has a good chance of getting hit. If they're going down they're fleeing, not eating.

Your approach speed will also dictate success. As a general rule, we have found that these fish have a tendency to say up earlier and later in the day, when the sun is at its lowest. That said, you'll generally have more time to come into a school during these conditions. Pay close attention to how finicky they get during the day. Are they shying away from the boat or going down if you're gunning in too hard? Is your approach too slow? Do the fish go down before you can get your offering into the mix? Will they eat anything you throw, or are they ultraselective? These are all factors to consider when chasing little tuna, and experimentation with approach, presentation, retrieve speed, line depth, and fly or lure selection all play a critical role in scoring.

Lure or fly selection depends on the bait being fed upon. It is highly unlikely that you'll see false albacore feeding on adult horse bunker. Rather, these fish tend to feed on smaller, slender baits such as spearing, rainfish (bay anchovies), and sand eels.

When fly fishing, smaller flies like Jiggies, Clouser Minnows, Skok Mushmouths, and Surf Candies stripped fast with a hand-over-hand retrieve tend to work best. At times it is not uncommon to find little tuna feeding on midsized baits like peanut bunker and mullet. Here Bucktail Deceivers and Baby Angel flies would be a better choice. We prefer to use longer, 6- to 8-foot fluorocarbon leaders, because these fish have tremendous eyesight. Nothing less than a 9-weight fly rod will do, and fly reels need to be large arbor and saltwater corrosion resistant. Make sure your fly reel is spooled with sufficient backing as well. One hundred fifty yards of 30-pound micron or 30-pound hi-vis PowerPro should be used.

For spin tactics, small metals such as Deadly Dicks, Ava 007s, Crippled Herring, and Hopkinses all work well. In addition to metals, soft baits like Slug-Gos or Fin-S fish prove deadly when rigged Carolina style, using a hook whose point goes back into the soft belly of the bait and is ripped across the surface with no additional weight. Try to tie everything direct when fishing for these football-shaped speedsters. They have very keen eyesight, and going direct with limited terminal tackle on your spinning and conventional rods will give you the advantage. We will use a 6-foot 20-pound fluorocarbon leader that is tied to the main line via a double uniknot. For the main line, we prefer the new braids like PowerPro or Stren Super Braid. These lines are Spectra fibers that have absolutely no stretch at all and offer anglers to ability to use higher-pound-test lines that have very small diameters. Thirty-pound PowerPro has the same diameter as most 10-pound monofilaments. From the boat, we like to use 7- to 71/2-foot St. Croix rods that offer stiff butts for lifting power and fast tips for casting distance. For reels, you don't have to go ultraheavy; any of the 4000 Series reels from Shimano or the Okuma Inspira 45 would be a good choice.

There will also be those days when these little tunas do not show on the surface at all. We have seen many days when boats will pass up a productive area simply because they do not see surface action. One of the best ways to locate these fish when visual signs are not present is to troll light tackle. In addition to being a tremendous amount of fun, inshore trolling for little tunas can make the difference between having fish and not having fish. Tackle for inshore trolling should be light, yet sturdy enough to handle quick, powerful bursts when the fish first take the lures from the trolling spread. To do this, we prefer to use reels that have lever drags. Lever drags enable anglers to set the reels to a specific "pounds of pressure" both in strike mode and in full mode. One of the high-end reel companies that have recently exploded on the scene here along the east coast is AVET Reels. AVET manufactures a conventional lever-drag reel to handle any situation. From inshore trolling for false albacore and bonito, to offshore trolling and chunking for giant tuna and marlin, AVET reels are quickly becoming a favorite for many hard-core charter captains. For inshore applications, the AVET SX and MX Models are the perfect match when rigged with a light trolling rod like the St. Croix Premier Saltwater Series.

Your trolling spread should consist of a four rod set up. The first two rods in the furthest aft rod holders (closest to the stern) can be flat lines running approximately twenty to thirty feet behind the boat. The second two rods are your long lines. These can either go in outriggers, or in your center gunnel rod holders. These lines should be run approximately fifteen to twenty feet behind your first lines.

Lure selections is generally small, and can be a combination of feathers, zuckers, spoons, and cedar plugs. Many days color will make all the difference, so be sure to carry a variety of light, neutral, and dark colors.

Generally we will troll between six and seven knots. Once the first rod goes off, troll for at least five to seven seconds more to see if any of the other rods hook up. Because these fish travel in packs, they have a tendency to ambush a trolling spread all at once.

THE MAIN EVENT: SUCCESS WITH STRIPERS AND BLUEFISH

When the striper and bluefish blitzes are on out along the outer beaches, everything changes. Getting your presentation deeper and moving slower will without a doubt hook the largest fish in the school. Many times as stripers attack a school of bait, smaller fish take the lead on the surface and subsurface, while the larger, more lethargic stripers lurk below in search of crippled and missed baits. Similarly, it is not

Fall is a great time to tangle with big stripers like this 45-pounder caught by Tom McGinley. Quigley

uncommon to find larger stripers feeding under a pack of wild bait-tearing bluefish. For this reason, we always prefer to get our offering down deep, even when the fish are on top. Sure, it's tremendous to see bass and blues taking flies and plugs off the surface; still, the thought of hooking into trophy-sized stripers by going deep will keep your blood boiling enough to avoid the obvious.

Stripers and bluefish can prove much more predictable that little tuna during the fall run. The reasoning here is that these fish tend to move much slower than tuna, and will stay with a school of bait through the evening as it moves down the coast on its southward migration path. Feeding patterns can be somewhat predictable as well once a pattern is developed. Earlier in fall here in New Jersey, we do best on the boat with these species during the early-morning hours, with pre- and postdawn being downright tremendous at times. Later in the season, however—during late fall and early winter—late-afternoon and early-evening feeding patterns seem to develop and become more consistent.

That is not to say that this is a direct science; it certainly is not. The main point of this discussion is that you should determine the feeding pattern of the day or night and try to fish those times. Major factors dictating these patters are water temperatures, wind directions, tides, and moon phases. A significant change in any one of these factors can offset or turn on the feed. We have experienced many falls where bass will come in and blitz on peanut bunker for days at a time, literally nonstop day and night. The day they turn off, everyone says, "Where did all the fish go?" They didn't go anywhere. How would you feel if you ate for three days straight? Time for a little break from eating, eh? Or maybe water temps have dropped considerably with a changing wind, bringing cold water inshore. Many times during the fall run, the consensus is that stripers simply pass us by as they head south. And this is true to some

Tip
Always keep a fishing log during fall to keep track of fish movements and behaviors. This will give you a good starting point when selecting a specific tactic or location. Be sure to record both the air and water temperatures, tide and moon phases, bait type present, and lures or flies that worked well for you during the action.

degree; more often than not during the fall run, however, these fish are moving east to west before they move south. As water temperatures cool and or moon phases change, fish move into the inshore feeding zones along our beaches from the deeper, warmer holding holes 3 to 8 miles off the coast.

Needless to say, when the action does happen, you want to be prepared. Boat anglers are without a doubt at a serious advantage over surf anglers in that they can move wherever the fish go. Before we get into a few tactics and techniques that are sure to score for you in your own boat, we would like to make one point. Always respect the space of surf and jetty anglers when the blitz is going on. If the action is tight to the beach or in and along the jetty pockets, do not drive your boat into the action and ruin the blitz for these shorebound anglers. Surf and jetty anglers will wait for a shot at fish all day long, watching the boats bail fish one after another. When it's finally their turn and the action busts wide open right in front of them, out of nowhere comes "the fleet" charging fast to ruin the day. Bottom line: Respect this space and do your best to work together.

FINDING FISH ON THE OPEN WATER

Finding fish from the boat in fall starts with being aware of feeding habits and bait presence. Fall fish are most always on the feed, and on the move. Looking for signs of feeding is usually the best way to score right off the bat. One simple technique: Find the working birds, and you've pretty much found the fish. True in most respects. But once you find the school, how should you fish it? Just as you would with working schools of little tuna, you want to be cautious when approaching breaking fish, or subsurface fish when they're feeding under birds. We always try to get upwind and upcurrent from feeding schools of stripers and blues and drift through with the engines off. This allows us to fish the school effectively without spooking them. It only takes one selfish angler to drive right into the feeding school with engines blaring to ruin it for all the other boats.

Even after the birds have gone down, keep fishing the area. Many times bass and blues will go deep and hold just after a massive surface-feeding blitz. We will always mark the school with GPS on the first drift to pinpoint its location; this way when the birds do go away, and the fish head subsurface, you can simply go back to the location and fish deeper. Always take wind and currents into consideration when backtracking toward a school of fish. Most GPS chart plotters today will draw "tracks" on the screen to show where the boat began and ended a drift. Utilizing these lines during the backtrack can be crucial in finding the school.

What happens if the school is moving or drifting with the tide? Here's where an awareness of current direction and wind speed comes into play. Fish will move with current and not wind. However, your boat will drift with the wind so long as it's stronger than the current. Some boats, such as flat-bottomed or modified-V hulls, will drift faster than other boats, such as deep Vs. In this scenario, many flat-bottomed or modified-V boat owners have began to use a drift sock or sea anchor in order to slow the drift, thus allowing anglers to fish in the holding zone longer. When there are no signs of life, smart anglers will always fish structures in the area that are known to hold fish and bait.

Tip

Canyon Blue Tackle, Brielle, NJ, (*www.canyonbluetackle.com*) will build custom spreader bars and daisy chains for all your inshore and offshore bluewater trolling needs.

11

Boat Success with Structure

So what happens when the birds aren't working? Or better yet, how about those days when you want nothing more than to get away from the crowds chasing the birds and find fish on your own? Locating and understanding bottom structure in your local area is the key to finding fish when the obvious signs do not prevail.

IDENTIFYING UNDERWATER STRUCTURE

Most anglers have no idea what lurks below them when they fish. Bait is drawn to structure, mainly for protection but also due to the fact that structure often holds nutrients such as plankton that baitfish feed on. Finding fish on structure takes patience, and this is where a good sonar or fishfinder comes into play. As we discussed in chapter 8, these machines paint a picture of the playing field down below, and in addition to finding fish and bait, they can tell you what contours and structures are in the area. This is subsurface fishing, and playing close attention to how depth relates to structure is very important.

What your fishfinder can't do is tell you if there are fish outside your boat sonar's radius. For this reason, it's always a good idea to fish a structure or area thoroughly before moving on. Start by circling the structure slowly to see if you mark fish or bait. When the reading is obtained, set up above the area and drift through, always calculating where you think the wind will cross with the current to ensure you drift over the correct spot.

Capt. Gene shows that fly fishing over bottom structure with sinking lines like the RIO T-14 will produce nice stripers all season long. Quigley

Many times during the past fall season, we would set up over a large body of bass. As we drifted through and dropped down our diamond jigs, we could actually see the line and jig trail on the fishfinder as it went into the depth. This makes fishing in this type of situation almost foolproof: You can put your presentation at the exact depth where the fish are holding. Most of the time, unfortunately, it's not that easy. One of the biggest challenges boat anglers face is fishing these underwater structures correctly.

Once you've found underwater structure that is holding fish, boat positioning becomes critical to hooking up. Simple common sense will tell you that if you aren't in the right zone, you can't catch the fish. Just as you used boat positioning to your advantage when fishing schools of breaking fish, you need to do the same when targeting underwater structure that's holding fish. We always like to get set upwind and upcurrent of the structure, then drift through. Your drift path here becomes critical. Should the wind and current take you on either side of the structure, chances are you will move on without ever knowing what kind of bite you could have had.

We like to use both GPS chart plotters and fishfinders when targeting nonvisible underwater ledges, reefs, or holes. Our chart plotter pinpoints the exact location of the structure by marking as a waypoint. Most high-quality chart plotters that use updatable software will paint a pretty good picture of bottom contours. This isn't enough, though. To cut down the margin of mechanical error, run the sounder or fishfinder at the same time to pinpoint where the bottom contours change and define the structure. This allows you to cross-reference both machines and mark your waypoints exactly on the plotter.

ANCHORING FOR SUCCESS

There may come a time when anchoring over structure becomes more effective than drifting over it. Take, for example, wreck fishing, chunking, or chumming. In these situations, anglers need to maintain one position in order to catch fish. Most of our summer is spent on the midshore lumps off the New Jersey coast, chumming for bluefish and small tuna. Here we use chum, cut baits, and in many cases live baits to draw fish off a particular structure and into our slick. Without a proper anchor, or better yet a proper boat position with the anchor set, our slick does not draw the same direct line to the structure—hence no fish. Many anglers simply get to a specific area and drop the hook. There is a definite science to anchor fishing, and the proper position will definitely put more fish on the line. Knowing how wind and current will affect your position will help you find the right spot to drop your hook.

When setting up on a distinct piece of structure like a wreck or ledge, you'll want the target to lie directly behind you, with the currents moving in that same direction. Because you'll be throwing chum and live baits to draw the fish to the surface, you'll have to leave enough room between your boat and your target for the baits to reach the fish. Getting the proper anchor set generally comes down to a happy medium of not being too far or too close. Line scope—the amount of

---

Tip

When jigging for deep-water stripers and blues, we like to use 30- to 50-pound braided lines like PowerPro or Stren Super Braid. These lines feature *no* stretch, along with a very thin diameter and high breaking strength. Braids let you feel every possible bounce or pickup on the bottom, allowing you to keep your jig in the strike zone longer than with regular monofilament. Set the hook with a short pull when the fish hits. Because the braid has no stretch, setting up big will rip the hook right out of the fish's mouth.

line you let out in relation to the water's depth—is the most critical part of the equation. As a general rule, most boats will let out at a five-to-one scope—that is, 5 feet of anchor line for every 1 foot of water depth. On rough-water days, however, a five-to-one scope often just won't do, and anglers will increase the line scope to seven to one, sometimes even ten to one. Same scenario on flat calm days.

Obviously, it's not necessary to scope out more line than you'll require. But what if you fish a small boat with limited anchor line room? There are two solutions. First, and probably the most obvious, is to carry long shots (200 feet or more) of additional anchor line in an outside container. This can become quite cumbersome, however, especially on a small boat where space is limited. Rather, we have employed a system of upgrading our anchor size, chain length, and chain weight in order to gain a stronger hold with considerably less scope or line. We always go up one size with our anchors from the recommended size. In addition, we use a considerable longer (up to 20 feet) and heavier chain to help keep the anchor secured and in position.

VISIBLE STRUCTURE

There are many structures, including jetty tips, reefs, and sandbars, that cannot be either viewed with the fishfinder or anchored on; you'll need to fish them by down-and-dirty boat maneuvering. Just as we do when fishing structure in and along the backwaters, you'll want to fish *with* the currents and rips to ensure that your offering is presented in a natural way. Very few spearing or sand eels swim freely and quickly against a strong rip or current, and striped bass, bluefish, and weakfish know enough to refuse a presentation that doesn't appear at least somewhat natural, particularly with artificial lures and flies. Putting the boat in this precarious position can sometimes present quite a challenge.

When fishing jetty tips from a boat, it's extremely important to understand that the rock outcroppings, or groins, do not just stop at the water's surface. These pilings tend to slope down into the water for quite a distance, creating an extremely viable habitat for fish but also a dangerous situation for boat handlers who don't know the waters. It's always smart to check the jetties you plan to fish at dead low tide. This will give you at least a minimal picture as to where the rocks draw into the surf, and for how long.

Surf is another major danger when fishing jetty tips from a boat. For the unassuming eye, the water around jetty tips looks no different

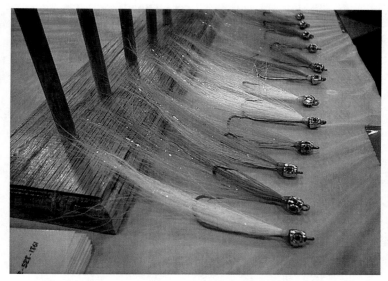

When fly fishing over structure weighted fleyes like Popovic's jiggies will help you get deep quickly. Freda

from any other part of the ocean. Even on the calmest of days, however, slow swells can push your vessel into or up on the rocks at a moment's notice. It's extremely important to understand how the surf affects structure when waves or swells are present. Never position your boat inside oncoming swells. When we work jetty tips the engine is always running, and one angler is always on the helm, paying close attention to distances to the visible or hidden rock croppings as well as to oncoming waves. Be sure to always tilt your engine up and truly know what your boat drafts.

That said, these areas are highly productive in spring, summer, and fall for trophy-sized striped bass. There are many ways to fish these areas; plug, spin, fly, and bait tactics will all have their moment in the sun. You will definitely want to get your offering as close to the rocks as humanly possible. Livelining baits like bunker or herring around these areas has produced some of the largest striped bass on the eastern seaboard.

Other notable structures that boat fishers find productive here in the Northeast are reefs and sandbars. These areas create an upwelling of sand or rock out in ocean waters and in many cases create rips that push water over these natural structures. Just as when you're boat fishing around jetty tips, be cautious when entering these areas. Current can move at an extremely fast pace and create dips or holes in the ocean's surface much like a rapid on a flowing river or stream. Stay above the turbulent or fast-moving water, again with one angler always operating the throttle and stemming the current. When done correctly, and timed right, captains can hold their boat in the exact same position for quite some time while stripers and bluefish gorge on baits like squid and herring.

> **Tip**
> When fishing jetty tips for resident stripers during summer months, try using topwater poppers to provoke a strike. Fish these areas just after sunup and right before sundown when winds are low and waters are calm. Cast the popper as close as possible to the tip or edge of the rock and work it with a slow and erratic retrieve.

Be sure to beef up your tackle when fishing in areas of fast or strong currents. Nine times out of 10 the fish will take off with the flow of the current, and you'll need to use all your might (and a strong rod) to bring them back to the boat. When fishing large, headstrong fish like striped bass and bluefish in currents, always keep your rod low to the water. The rod should never dip below your thighs and should also never come above your shoulders, especially in currents. This area of the body offers anglers the most leverage when fighting fish. Always let the rod work for you, by using the bottom half, or butt section, to do your lifting, steering, and down-and-dirty fighting.

Sandbars close to shore are often overlooked by boat anglers, simply because they tend to think bigger is always out deeper. This *can* be true, but remember that the world-record striped bass was plucked from the New Jersey surf by a wading angler, Al McReynolds, on the Vermont Avenue Jetty in Atlantic City, New Jersey. Sandbars close to shore are natural bait magnets, particularly for smaller baits like sand eels, peanut bunker, and rainfish. Baits are drawn up on and inside these bars for protection. Smaller boats in the 20- to 25-foot category can easily fish these inner bars as long as surf is at a minimum. As with jetty tip fishing, hopping sandbars can prove to be a dangerous game unless you're extremely familiar with the area and know how and when wave sets break on the bars. During groundswells, waves travel in for hundreds of miles in deeper water and begin to generate velocity as the water thins. Most waves will break in water that is half as deep as the wave is high; for this reason, sandbars become breaking points for swells that push in from sea. Boaters who stay on the outer bars in deeper water can effectively fish these areas from a casting distance away as long as they always have one eye on the swell.

What's great about these outer bars is that fish like striped bass, bluefish, and weakfish constantly cruise the edges looking for food. We know that the inside of the bar is considered the safe zone for baitfish. Here you will want to cast your offering up onto or beyond the bar and retrieve back into the deep water. This will without a doubt be your best chance to hook up with ambushing gamefish.

When all is said and done, learning to fish structure will undoubtedly make you a better anglers and put more fish on your line. Those who rely solely on working birds and visible blitzes will experience lulls way more than the angler who understands and can effectively fish structure.

12

Big-Game
Fly Fishing

Oneofthe challenges every salt-water angler should experience is fighting a *really* big fish. We're not talking big bass, bluefish, or weakfish, mind you. We're talking tuna. Tuna are considered some of the most powerful gamefish in the sea, and many anglers across the globe have dedicated much of their lives to the pursuit of these wonderful creatures.

There are many different types of tuna; in fact, all tuna are actually part of the mackerel family. Here along the northeastern seaboard, four species of tuna make up most of the catches: yellowfin, bluefin, bigeye, and longfin (albacore). For our discussion in this book, however, we will concentrate on tactics for the most popular, the bluefin and yellowfin. Catching these creatures on trolling and standup tackle is quite a treat, but what if we were to tell you that we prefer to target these fish with fly tackle? Crazy, huh? Hardly.

To date, many fly anglers have had great success with taking tuna under 200 pounds on fly tackle. Most notable has been Brad Kistler's 196-pound bluefin, taken off Cape Lookout, North Carolina, aboard Captain Bill Harris's *Fly Caster*. In addition to these larger, more powerful tuna, fly anglers also have had great success targeting smaller "schoolie" bluefin, Atlantic bonito, false albacore, dorado, white marlin, and skipjack tuna in and along the offshore waters of the Northeast.

FINDING FISH ON THE OFFSHORE GROUNDS

Every summer the waters referred to as the "northeast canyons" come alive with pelagic species that are massive in both size and numbers.

Offering everything from skipjack tuna to giant blue marlin, these off-shore canyons rank as some of the best saltwater fishing destinations in the world. The Hudson Submarine Canyon, which lies approximately 70 miles east of the New Jersey coast, draws hundreds of big-game anglers from around the globe to fish in its target-rich waters.

The Hudson Canyon is an ancient extension of New York's Hudson River Valley, which stretches more than 400 nautical miles seaward from the New York/New Jersey Harbor, across the continental margin, to the deep ocean basin. A long, deep trench made up of a series of holes, lumps, wrecks, and ridges begins off New York Bight's Hudson River and stretches southeast across the Jersey Shore directly to the Hudson Canyon.

When summer's high-pressure weather systems prevail along the East Coast, these waters remain alive with pelagic gamefish, offering fly anglers consistent action. As with most saltwater fisheries, proper tactics and timing can make the difference between a marginal trip and a glorious one. Here along the New Jersey coast we have world-class tuna fishing from late July through early November.

Tip

Heading offshore can be a dangerous game if you are not prepared for or familiar with the waters. Always head to sea with an experienced captain before taking the journey yourself. Be sure to have all your emergency lifesaving equipment in tip-top shape. Major safety equipment on board should include a life raft, Class 1 life jackets, EPIRB, flares, horn, advanced first-aid equipment, handheld GPS and radio (as backups to your onboard electronics), extra food and water, fire extinguishers, and survival suits.

On any given day during New Jersey's offshore tuna bite, anglers can fly fish for multiple species of tuna both large and small. These fork-tailed speedsters perform line-screaming runs that will test the skills and tackle of even the most seasoned anglers. Like all members of the mackerel family, tuna are highly migratory fish, and they can travel at speeds upward of 40 miles an hour. During late spring and early summer, these fish all travel the same migrational paths up the Gulf Stream and take residence off the Northeast Coast.

School bluefin in the thirty- to sixty-pound range provide flyrodders tremendous action from late summer through early fall in the Mudhole. Quigley

Finding tuna with fly tackle on the offshore grounds is a whole other world from chasing the smaller "little tuna" along the inshore beaches. Unlike the up-and-down feeding frenzies that that occur along our beachfronts with false albacore and bonito every fall, these same fish feed and react differently out on the open water. Offshore, the bulk of the feeding takes place below the surface, requiring anglers to rely on their abilities to correlate underwater structure, feeding habits, and today's fish-finding technology.

Given the ocean's expansive landscape, finding locations offshore that hold fish becomes the most challenging task. Underwater structure, water temperatures, water clarity, and the presence of baitfish all play important roles in holding fish in this area. Having a quality fishfinder and chart-plotting GPS enables savvy anglers to quickly determine where to begin. Today's satellite technology and Web sites that offer sea-surface temperatures and water movements are superior fishfinding tools that can be used days before a trip. On these Web sites, anglers can download up-to-the-minute satellite-based information on sea-surface temperatures, tidal movements, temperature breaks, and current speeds and directions. They also give the exact latitude and longitude GPS and loran numbers. Once you've located your target area, it's best to check throughout the evening and just before you depart the dock to ensure that favorable conditions still prevail.

GETTING TUNA TO THE BOAT

When you arrive at the fishing grounds, you'll need to decide whether to anchor or drift. Nine times out of 10, anchoring above the targeted structure will produce the best results. A drifting technique will prove effective when you plan to work a larger area of subtle underwater formations in light winds and slow currents.

When you've decided to anchor, knowing how wind and current will affect your position will help you find the right spot to drop your hook. When setting up on a distinct piece of structure like a wreck or ledge, you'll want the target to lie directly behind you, with the currents moving in that same direction. Because you'll be throwing chum and live baits to draw the fish to the surface, you'll have to leave enough room between your boat and your target for the baits to reach the fish. Once your position is secure, it's time to start your slick.

It's not entirely unlikely to see tuna feeding on the surface off-shore, and when you do you'll want to take advantage of the gift and get on the fish right away. Here traditional cast-and-retrieve fly fishing becomes the best tactic. If you've ever experienced the speed of false albacore or bonito tearing up bait along inshore beaches, multiply that by 10 and you'll understand how fast bluefin and yellowfin move on a pod of bait. For this type of fly fishing, you will need to work as a team, with one angler always on the helm while the other is in position to cast. Most of the time in the offshore canyons, however, these fish hold deep on structure, and alternative tactics are used to bring fish within casting range. Drawing tuna to the surface requires throwing a menu of chum baits over the side of the boat. We have found the best technique to be a combination of cut baits like butterfish and sardines, fresh spearing, and, most importantly, live bait.

Most conventional-tackle canyon fishers use only cut butterfish as their main attractant in the slick. For fly anglers, however, we have found that working smaller inshore baits like fresh spearing and live peanut bunker into the mix produces the best results. There are two critical reasons why this tactic is more practical. During the traditional butterfish-chunking situation, tuna key in on drifting chunk bait, which creates a selective environment where the fish will feed only on those specific chunk baits. As fly fishers, we have the rewarding challenge of tricking our prey into taking imitated baits. By using smaller spearing and live peanut bunker, we can create a feeding atmosphere that initiates two key factors: predators that aggressively chase their prey and tuna eating smaller offerings that better resemble the true profile of a slender bait or fly.

> **Tip**
> Before you head offshore, be sure to check the NOAA offshore marine forecast starting 48 hours prior, then 24 hours prior, then 12 hours, then right before you leave. Try to leave your itinerary with a close friend or relative before you go. For novice bluewater anglers, it's always best to head out with a partner boat. Be sure to perform a complete all-points check on your vessel just before you leave the dock, and always go out with a full tank of fuel.

During the beginning stages of the slick, we tend to chum heavily with fresh spearing and lightly with live peanut bunker in order to preserve the live baits until the tuna arrive. Once they do, transition to a lighter dash of spearing and a slightly increased offering of live bait, which creates chaos around the boat and turns selective tuna into frenzied feeding machines. It's important to throw your baits all around the boat randomly. Dropping the baits in the same spot behind the stern will carry your offerings in a regulated path that allows fish to hold deeper in the slick.

Once the slick has been established, the name of the game is patience. If the fish don't show up right away, you have to stick to your decision to fish that particular area. We've seen anglers leave their slick after an hour or two of chumming, only to find that the bite busted wide open just after the tide changed. The best scenario for tuna fly fishing in this situation is to have one or two anglers fishing the slick and another working the chum baits. Any pause in your chumming can easily push the fish back out of casting range, or out of the scene entirely.

FLY FISHING WITH THE RIGHT SETUP

Two factors will determine your fly-line selections for the day. First is how fast the currents take the fly back into the slick. Stronger currents and winds will mean starting with a faster-sinking line. The second factor is how deep the fish are feeding. Strong currents don't necessarily mean the fish won't feed in the upper water column, and finding the sweet spot will make all the difference in the world. We usually start by using 350-grain sinking line. If we still cannot reach the depths desired, we then move to a heavier sinking line like Rio's T-14. At times, floating or intermediate lines can yield favorable results, so you'll want to be prepared with a wide variety of lines.

As in all fly-fishing situations, presentation is key. The flies you present in the slick should look exactly like the baits. If the tuna are keyed in on fresh spearing, then slender-profiled flies like the Surf Candy or Jiggy will work best. Keep the retrieves slow and erratic. In some situations, the best technique is to not move the fly at all, but rather let it swing back into the slick. When live peanut bunker turn on the bite, we prefer Baby Angel and Bucktail Deceiver flies and a very rapid two-handed retrieve that emulates scared baits in search of shelter. Since the water is crystal clear most of the time, we like flies tied in the exact colors of the baits, with a flashy, translucent appearance. Tuna can straighten many brands of saltwater fly hooks with a single surge. For this reason, we use specific saltwater fly-tying hooks, and conventional saltwater tuna hooks to tie our flies with. For smaller bluefin and yellowfin, we prefer the Varivas 990 and the Tiempco 600SP in sizes 4/0 and up. When smaller hooks are required to imitate smaller baits, the Owner Gorilla live-bait hook is our go-to hook for flies such as Surf Candies, Clousers, Deceivers, and Baby Angels. When larger flies and hooks are needed, we use the Mustad Sea Demon big-game hooks. Circle hooks, like the Owner Muta Hook, are used when drifting chunk flies like Captain Gene Quigley's Foam Butterfish Chunk and Dave Frassinelli's Bloody Chunk back into the slick.

As you can imagine, your fly tackle will need to the best of the best. Small bluefin and yellowfin under 75 pounds can be handled well on a 12- or 13-weight, while larger tunas in the 75- to 200-pound range should be fought with nothing less than a 14-weight. The Cape Fear Rod Company has developed a one-piece, 8-foot 17/19-weight rod designed especially for tuna over 100 pounds. This is probably one the finest lifting tool for big fish on the market today. When tuna present themselves on the surface as described earlier in this chapter, a 12-weight fly rod, like St. Croix's 12-weight Ultra Legend, will be a better choice since it offers both castability and significant lifting power.

You need heavy fly rods and strong reels to tangle with offshore tunas.
Quigley

Having the right rod for the situation is the first critical part to the big-game tackle situation. The fly reel, however, can make or break a fight with a big tuna. Reels need to have superstrong drags, be mechanically flawless, and be able to hold at least 500 yards of 50-pound micron backing. We have never seen tuna of less than 80 pounds take more than 300 yards of backing, but you can rest assured that a bluefin or yellowfin over the 100-pound mark will use every bit of that and then some, especially while you're fishing the deep-water canyons of the Northeast. Ted Juracsik's Billy Pate's Bluefin and the Tibor Pacific are two reels that we have come to trust day in and day out for offshore fly fishing. These reels are machined with superior technology and have silky-smooth drags that could stop a truck.

Leaders need to be perfect. The slightest nick or improperly tied knot can cause the leader to fail at any time during the long, strenuous fight. There are two types of leader systems to use: leaders for non-IGFA records, and those for IGFA class-tippet records. IGFA leaders must conform to generally accepted fly-fishing customs. A leader includes a class tippet and, optionally, a shock tippet. A butt or taper section between the fly line and the class tippet is also considered part of the leader, and there are no limits on its length, material, or strength. A class tippet must be made of nonmetallic material and attached either directly to the fly or to the shock tippet if one is used.

The class tippet must be at least 15 inches long (measured inside connecting knots). With respect to knotless, tapered leaders, the terminal 15 inches will also determine tippet class. There is no maximum length limitation. A shock tippet, not to exceed 12 inches in length, may be added to the class tippet and tied to the fly. It can be made of any type of material, and there is no limit on its breaking strength. The shock tippet is measured from the eye of the hook to the single strand of class tippet and includes any knots used to connect the shock tippet to the class tippet.

On our boats, we traditionally use non-IGFA leader systems unless our clients ask for them. Our tuna leaders are simple. Depending on the size of the fish, we will employ an 8- to 9-foot straight shot of 20- to 60-pound fluorocarbon that has a Bimini twist loop at the top to form a loop-to-loop connection with the fly line. This is then tied directly to the fly via a uniknot or palomar knot. Should we require a bite tippet of 80 to 100 pounds, it's connected to the main leader via a Bimini twist/Curcione speed nail knot connection.

FIGHTING TUNA ON FLY TACKLE

Fighting a tuna on fly tackle requires strength, agility, stamina, and, most importantly, technique. For the most part, all tuna fight in a similar manner. Whether they are 20 pounds or 200, you can expect the same dance—except the 200-pounder will dance with you for hours.

When the bite happens, set the hook with authority. Use a series of sharp strip strikes to ensure that the hook is set well. During the first run, let the fish go without any interruptions other than side pressure from the rod. Never point the rod tip directly at the fish, but instead keep it low and off to the side between waist and shoulder level. This initial run is pure excitement, and it's about the only time you'll see the tuna swim in an outward motion close to the surface. A word of caution during the initial stages of the fight: Never adjust the drag, especially if you have a bigger fish on. We set the drag before the fight begins at a minimal pressure of about 4 to 5 pounds.

After the first or second explosive run, the fish will sound. Now the fun begins. At this point, anglers should increase the drag slightly to around 7 to 9 pounds of pressure (depending on tippet size) so the lifting process can work effectively. With your rod low to the water, begin to pump the fish up to the surface by performing a series of short lifting strokes up, then make a quick gain of the line with the reel back down. Keep your knees bent and your upper body and back centered over your torso. The minute you straighten your legs and hunch forward, the tuna gains the initiative.

When the fish gets its first glimpse of the boat, be prepared for a quick, powerful surge back into the depths. As the fish tires, it will start to swim in a deep circular motion that can take you around the boat on what we call the "tuna tango." This circular swimming motion will start with large, wide circles and then decrease to small tight circles as the fight winds down. Once the tuna breaks the surface during the circular motion, it's pretty safe to sink the gaff

New Jersey fall tuna caught by Pete DeStefano in the Mudhole. Quigley

into the fish. Always go for a head shot first; you'll spoil the meat by sinking a steel object into the center portion of the body. New Jersey local tuna angler Dean Nelson put it best when he described catching bluefin tuna on the fly: "There simply are *no* other fish."

The Guide's Approach—
Techniques and Strategies

13

Presentation Theory

Whenever we're out on the water, one of the most frequently asked questions from our clients is, "What artificial do you select to catch fish?" Most of the time the answer is simple—"Match the hatch," to steal a phrase from the freshwater world. But what about those times when the bait may not be so obvious or a wide variety is present? How do you decide then?

Luckily for us, the feeding behaviors of our inshore species are not limited to the real thing. Instead, our inshore species are more than willing to attack a wide variety of artificial offerings. It is for this reason that catching fish has not become an exact science and most anglers can enjoy a great deal of success.

There are, however, going to be those times when you would think the exact opposite is true. Fish are there, but they won't hit a thing. At these times, lure selection can be critical, especially when fish are keyed in on particular bait. As we search through our tackle box or surf bag, questions like *What size?* and *What color will work best at a particular location or time of day?* go through our heads. We can complicate these questions further by adding *What tide, What water temperature, What moon phase, What current, What wind, What wave condition*s . . . the list could go on and on.

To answer all these questions takes years of experience on the water and keeping mental notes or written logs to match results with conditions. But we can simplify matters by focusing in on three main questions that set the foundations for success. These would be what we call CPR for the angler: color, profile, and retrieve, also known as presentation.

Each and every time we select an artificial, we have to decide on its color, its size or profile, and how we will present it. Which one of these three components is most important to success?

RETRIEVE

Your retrieve or presentation is the main key to your success when it comes to catching fish. Sure, we've all seen one particular artificial become hot for some reason, and everyone runs to the tackle shop to get his hands on one. Many anglers quickly get a false sense of confidence, thinking that because they now have the right artificial, success is imminent.

Maybe not, though, even if you have the right size and right color in the water. If your artificial doesn't behave like the real thing, then good luck, because you're going to need it. Here's where knowing your bait's behavior is critical. In other words, do you know how and at what speed your bait normally moves through the water? Does it remain high or low in the water column, or at mid-depths? Does it change direction quickly or is it a methodical in nature? Can it swim against a current or is it swept around? All these behaviors will factor into how you make your presentation.

> **Tip**
> Sometimes an unnatural-looking retrieve may produce strikes, because it stands out as different. Often it is interpreted as a territorial threat. Other times—particularly when fish are blitzing—no retrieve at all will work. As your artificial just lies there and gets pushed around, fish will take it for a stunned or injured bait and strike.

For instance, a fly fisher presenting a meticulously reproduced crab pattern for bass during the summer soft-shell season will not draw strikes with a quick two-handed retrieve. A motion like this is unnatural, and even the dumbest fish of the bunch will shy away. We doubt very much if bass are accustomed to seeing crabs swim at them.

Thus you need to learn how your bait behaves and moves, and be able to replicate this. Only then will your imitation will be effective. In the case of our crab pattern, a strip–pause slow retrieve on or near the bottom is important. Small crabs are feeble swimmers and are at the mercy of strong currents and rough surf when not buried in the sand.

Let's look at another case that many anglers are more familiar with or have experienced first-hand. This time we move to a fall peanut bunker blitz, when bass are busting through the pods of bait. Fish are clearly visible and only a short cast in front of you. But despite the blitz conditions, it's common to walk away frustrated after casting directly into the school, without even a hookup.

In this scenario, your presentation would have to be altered to fish the outskirts of the school, away from the "safety in numbers" phenomenon, or to fish below the school imitating an injured bait falling to the bottom. While not foolproof, these two presentation methods are much more attractive to an opportunistic bass looking for an easy meal.

Big bulky flies and a fast jerky retrieve are often the correct presentation for gator blues on the fly. Client Murray Dalziel landed this 13-pounder on board with Capt. Jim Freda. Freda

COLOR

Following presentation, the other two considerations to look at when selecting an artificial are color and profile. Let's look at color first, and let's start by examining color perception from the fish's perspective.

The majority of the saltwater fish targeted by inshore anglers have the ability to see colors. They do not, however, see colors with the same perception that we are accustomed to. This is due to differences in the anatomical makeup of the eye. Research tells us that these inshore species have a keen ability to detect movement and the ability to distinguish objects against specific backgrounds rather than to perceive precise details and colors. In fact, we will never know what fish's perception actually is because we will never know for sure how their brains process stimuli from their color receptors—the cones found in the fish's eye.

Take the striped bass. We have all encountered times when one particular color is definitely more effective than others. We make mental notes of this and keep using this artificial as our "go-to" lure. Our mental notes will also include but are not limited to when this color works, day or night, dawn or dusk, time of year; conditions in which it works, rough or calm; and how it's being retrieved. As captains and guides, being out on the water all the time gives us a distinct advantage in logging the many different events and the colors that were most effective.

> **Tip**
> During the day when surf conditions are rough and there's a lot of whitewater, a black artificial will stand out better by presenting more of a contrast against the white foam.

We also need to look at how the physical properties of water affect colors and their effectiveness. In the visible spectrum, different colors of light will penetrate to different depths. Reds are usually filtered out in the first 10 yards of the water column; blue and greens penetrate the deepest. Thus, what colors of light are available to be backscattered or reflected from an artificial ultimately depends on what depth the artificial is being retrieved at. The color of the artificial that we see before it goes into the water is not the same as what's viewed underwater by a fish.

In clear, shallow water, the artificial we see in our hand will look much the same to the fish. In deep, turbid, or discolored water, however, colors will be altered considerably. Here colors such as white, yellow, and chartreuse will produce best, because they do reflect the minimal amounts of light that are present below the surface.

Other factors to consider when deciding on a particular color are the use of prismatic or holographic tapes and high-tech fluorescent paints. In flies, synthetic flash materials such as Flashabou, Krystal Flash, Angel Hair, Sparkle Flash, tinsel, and Lite-Bright can be added. All these materials will help scatter light from the artificial to the fish's eye in much the way that the silvery prismatic stripes or ultratranslucent scales of a fish's body do.

PROFILE

When referring to size of an artificial, we prefer the term *profile*. A bait-fish's profile is three dimensional: It has length, width, and height. When large baits such as blueback herring or adult bunker are present, a big artificial will fit the bill. Six to 10 inches in length, 2 to 3 inches high, and ½ to 1 inch wide will produce the biggest fish. It would most likely be unproductive to cast small 2- to 3-inch artificials when the fish are keyed in on bigger baits.

Keep in mind also that your artificial's profile will appear differently to a predator from different viewing perspectives. In water 2 to 3 feet deep, for instance, the fish will be viewing your artificial from eye-level perspective. In this instance, the fish will not be able to perceive the dimension of width (girth). But the dimensions of length and height will be clearly evident.

A wide variety of baits is found along the coast that can vary in color, profile, and movement. (L-r, top to bottom: squid, porgy, peanut bunker, spearing, mullet, baby bluefish.) Freda

When fishing the upper part of the water column over deep water, your artificial will most likely be viewed from below, so width (girth) becomes more important whereas height is less so. In this situation, length is still perceptible and is important.

Fly fishers can zero in on an imitation's profile by using many of the synthetic lightweight materials on the market today. Materials such as Bozo Hair, Kinky Fiber, Angel Hair, Super Hair, and Big Fly Fiber don't absorb water readily and will breathe in the water, lending the illusion of a wide-bodied bait. These lightweight materials also make it easier to cast bigger flies with less effort. Don't overlook natural materials for wide-bodied imitations, though: Bucktails and feathers will always be important to the fly tier, as will the tying procedure used to build the correct profile.

So which characteristic is more important when you're making your selection, color or profile? If we had to choose, we'd opt for the correct profile first. Here's why. The majority of our inshore species are opportunistic feeders. Bass in particular will strike quickly if the situation presents itself. The competition factor plays a key role here in their aggressive nature. That's why the majority of bass that you hook will hit hard. They have made up their minds and go for it.

A correct profile will be more of a stimulus than will color since under different conditions colors can be masked. Remember, the colors we see as we hold the artificial in our hand are different from what a bass sees. Form and movement of the artificial are key.

14

Fishing
Live Bait

Livelining is a simple and exciting way to fish, and it will increase every angler's chance of catching that trophy fish. Generally, your live bait will do most of the work for you. Just find some structure, properly hook the bait, drop it to the bottom, and wait for a strike.

There are several good ways to present live bait, including fishfinder rig; a rig with a three-way swivel; rubber-core sinkers with a swivel; or a swivel, leader, and hook. Most livelining situations will involve no weight at all, but if you're working areas with current or significant depth, using weight is the favorite method for getting your live bait within sight of holding fish at a particular depth. Pay close attention to how fast the current is moving. This will determine the proper amount of weight to keep your bait swimming naturally and along the bottom.

Client Rich Karpowicz lands a fish of a lifetime, a 58-pound striper on board with Capt. Gene Quigley, June 10, 2004. Quigley

One good way to add weight is with an egg sinker fishfinder rig. This is a simple rig to construct; all you need is two barrel swivels, an egg sinker, and a treble hook. Tie a swivel to the main line; then tie a 15-inch leader (40-pound test) thread onto the egg sinker, tie on the next swivel and another shorter length of leader (10 to 12 inches), and finally add the treble hook. A good hook is the Eagle Claw 1/0 L774 laser-sharp bronze hook.

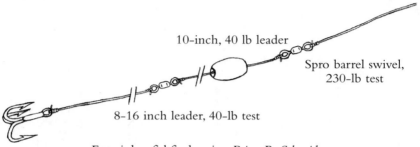

10-inch, 40 lb leader

Spro barrel swivel, 230-lb test

8-16 inch leader, 40-lb test

Egg sinker fishfinder rig. *Brian R. Schneider*

Another method for livelining with weight is using a standard three-way swivel rig. Attach 4 to 6 inches of light leader as a dropper; if you get hung up in the rocks, the sinker will break away.

Hook live bait in front of the dorsal fin, so steering is easy. Conventional tackle is preferred, along with 20- to 40-pound mono line. Over the past several years, we have switched over to 50-pound braided super lines, which offer less resistance in the water, as well as more power and strength to move fish away from rocks.

LIVELINING HERRING

One of the early live-bait choices, from the end of April through early June, is the alewife (*Alosa pseudoharengus*), the most abundant spring herring. This species is often confused with the blueback herring (*A. aestivalis*). The blueback herring has, as you might expect, a blue back, while the alewife's back is grayish green. The eyes of the alewife are also larger in diameter than the snout length, whereas the eyes of the blueback are smaller—usually equal in diameter to its snout length. Both species average about 12 inches in length and weigh from 8 to 16 ounces.

Nothing in the world gets a striped bass angler more excited than having a 30-pound striper explode on a livelined herring. You must

When live lining use off-set hooks. Make sure the hook point is riding up. This will eliminate hooks turning back into the bait. Caris

anticipate when to strike and set the hook. If the hookset occurs when the bait isn't yet fully in the fish's mouth, all you'll have for your efforts is a severely damaged bait.

How to Catch Herring

The laws in your area will determine how you are allowed to catch herring. During the season, cast nets, dip nets, herring darts, and Sabiki rigs are some of the productive choices. When using a single herring dart in lakes or tidal areas, we prefer to use 4-pound-test mono, although there are times when scaling down to 2-pound test—which is almost totally invisible in water—can catch you a few more herring.

A good level of care should be used to ensure that your baits remain healthy and frisky. Maintaining a slime coating is critical for their safe transportation to the fishing grounds; removing the slime is fatal. Keep your hands wet when handling the baits. One advantage of using herring is that they can tolerate fresh water.

Fishing Herring

Casting a live herring—or any live bait—is not recommended. These fish have never even felt their own weight; flinging them 30 yards through the air will surely leave them stunned or killed.

The proper way to fish a herring is to place it in the water quickly after positioning the hook in its back. Hook live bait in front of the dorsal fin with an offset-style hook. The hook point should be riding up. The newly hooked herring will have some level of fear as it tries to swim away from the tension of the hook. With a hook positioned correctly, you can steer the herring away from land toward the drop-off or other feeding zone. Although we have been fishing these live baits for more than 40 years, we still look forward to the livelining season with great anticipation every spring.

LIVELINING BUNKER

Live adult menhaden are another preferred live bait for trophy striped bass. *Brevoortia tyrannus*, commonly known as bunker or menhaden, are members of the herring family and migrate up the coast from Florida to the Northeast in spring and early summer.

Bunker are strong baitfish. With a good supply of salt water, they can be kept in the same live wells as other herrings. Aeration is critical, however, because these fish never stop swimming, and they burn up a lot of energy and oxygen. Still, these durable live baits will survive much longer than other herring under the same conditions.

Catching Bunker

Spring and summer are the best times to locate live adult bunker. If you can reach them from shore or approach them by boat, a cast net is right for the job. From shore or in shallow water, a standard 6-foot cast net with ⅜- to ½-inch mesh works perfectly. These nets have approximately 1 pound of lead per foot.

When menhaden holding in deeper water approached by boat, we recommend a cast net designed to sink fast, one that has larger holes and heavier weights. For deep water, nets with 1½ pounds of lead per foot are appropriate. The performance of the net is important because you may only get one shot at the bunker. Sometimes netting them from a boat takes skill. Try to approach the school quietly and turn off the engines when the boat is positioned to drift over them.

At times, a cast net will be ineffective because the bunker may be too easily spooked or the school may keep its distance from the boat. The school may be also holding farther from shore if you're on foot. This is where the bunker snag comes into play.

Snatch hooks or "bunker snags" are weighted treble hooks that come in a range of sizes. They can be used to snag baits and transfer them into your live well. On the other hand, you can cast into a school

This 34-lb trophy bass fell for a live bunker fished by Capt. Jim. Freda

of bunker, snag one, and let it sit. Many times schools of bass are under them waiting for an opportunity. There is usually more bait than predators, so if you're having no luck, simply move on to another pod.

To liveline a bunker, hook it crosswise through the flesh, about ½ inch deep, just in front of the dorsal fin. Penetrating too deep in the flesh can destroy the bait.

Bunker can be fished from jetties, at inlets, and along the beach. Many liveliners pass up the surf in favor of jetties. Under the right conditions of calm surf and offshore winds, however, fishing live bunker directly from the beach can get you good results.

Hooks: Live bait hooks are an extremely important part of the liveliner's equipment. It is essential that these hooks be very strong, very sharp and most important have an offset point. We like to use the Gamakatsu Octopus style #02017 hook in the size range 7/0 to 10/0. These hooks are chemically sharpened and razor sharp right out of the box. Using these hooks, you will have exceptional success and increased hook ups.

> ### Tip
> You can improve a weighted treble rig by snelling a series of two to three 1/0 unweighted treble hooks on the leader approximately 12 to 14 inches apart. These smaller unweighted hooks will do less damage to the bait and increase your chances of snagging a live bait.

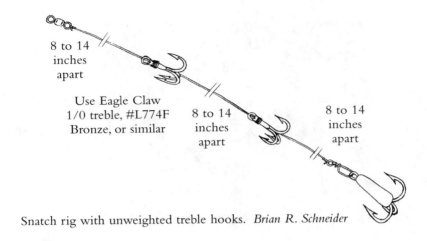

8 to 14
inches
apart

Use Eagle Claw
1/0 treble, #L774F
Bronze, or similar

8 to 14
inches
apart

8 to 14
inches
apart

Snatch rig with unweighted treble hooks. *Brian R. Schneider*

Using Live Peanut Bunker

Using live peanut bunker is great fun. In autumn these fish migrate along the beach as they come out of our back bays and rivers. They can be cast-netted rather easily, allowing you to take as many baits as needed. If you have a boat, huge schools of peanut bunker can be found just outside a sandbar or farther offshore. Jetties, submerged rock piles, ledges, and channels are all good places to liveline peanut bunker.

LIVELINING EELS

Most veteran striped bass anglers will tell you that nothing compares to live using eels when it comes to catching trophies. Most bait shops along the coast carry a nice supply of live eels. We prefer to purchase eels that are 11 to 13 inches in length. Eels of this size allow us to fish a variety of conditions. Eels in the 8- to 10-inch size, though effective, do not afford the flexibility to fish a variety of surf conditions. Simply put, you cannot cast them into a strong southeast wind, which we sometimes choose to do.

Many times our local bait shops are out of live eels, especially when the fishing gets hot. So you might want to give potting a try. Getting started is simple; all you need is a few eel pots or minnow traps, and both work well.

Crushed clams or mussels are the baits of choice. (In the past, before they were protected, crushed horseshoe crabs were popular because their scent is extremely attractive to eels.) Since eels are nocturnal, you will have the best success setting your pots in the evening hours and retrieving them at dawn.

Seashore lakes are good places to locate eels, as are lagoons, rivers, and back bays. Set your eel pots in water that is no more than 4 to 6 feet deep. Spring and early summer are the best times of year to pot. Concentrate your efforts during this time to store up your year's supply.

Keeping eels alive and healthy doesn't require a tremendous amount of effort. Serious eel anglers will keep hundreds alive in a wooden eel cart floating in a lagoon or bay all season long. Most anglers keep them in a 5-gallon bucket, preferably black, which turns the eels jet black—the best color for fishing them live or rigged. The bucket should have enough water to keep them moist. The eels will take oxygen from the surface to survive. If there is too much water in the bucket, the eels will drown without adequate aeration.

A friend of ours has another neat way to care for eels—a three-bucket system that keeps them alive for days. Here are the details. The buckets must fit inside each other and be easy to separate. Start with a 5-gallon bucket that will fit in your fish cooler. (Use large white marine coolers.) This bucket will carry the eels, so it should be black to keep them dark. Next comes a smaller 2-gallon bucket with 30 to 40½-inch holes drilled in the bottom. Fill a second 2-gallon bucket about a third of the way with ice. Place this ice bucket on top of the eels; the ice water will drain and keep the eels lethargic. Also, keep a small block of wood in the bottom of the largest bucket so the eels do not drown in the drip water.

Carrying Your Eels

Carry your eels in an eel bag. This is nothing more than a mesh bag (dive bag) with a drawstring top. Depending where we fish, we sometimes add a small length of rope so the eel bag can rest in the water while we fish. This method works well for areas like Turtle Cove or Montauk. When fishing jetties, we either shorten up the bag so the eels stay above the knee or transport them in a 5-gallon bucket. When using the shorter bag, remember to wet the eels so they don't dry out and die.

Eel Hooks and Leaders

We prefer to use a 5/0 Octopus-style Gamakatsu hook snelled on a 24- to 36-inch piece of 30-pound-test leader material. Attach a 230-pound-test number 2 Spro barrel swivel. These swivels are nice because they feature extra strength for their small size. When fishing rocky areas, use a 40-pound leader.

Hook eels through their lower jaw and out through the center of their nose. If you've ever tried this with a frisky eel, you know it can be quite a challenge. This is where a mesh eel bag comes in handy by providing you better grip. Slide the eel out the top of the bag so only the head is exposed. Grip the eel tight and hook as described above. As soon as you pull the eel out of the bag, get it in the water; this way it won't have the chance to ball up on the leader.

> **Tip**
> Hooks are extremely important part of the liveliner's equipment. It's essential that livelining hooks be very strong, be very sharp, and—most importantly—have an offset point. We like to use the Gamakatsu Octopus-style 02017 hook in sizes 7/0 through 10/0. These hooks are chemically sharpened and razor sharp out of the box.

There are many ways to fish live eels in the surf. In tidal water or swift current, we generally cast upcurrent and let the eel drift naturally along the bottom. Although this is very effective, there are times when eels should be fished similarly to plugs. Cast and retrieve your eel as if it were a plug, but make the retrieve extremely slow: After every crank, wait three to five seconds, then repeat.

The location you fish will determine the speed of your retrieve. A deep jetty tip with a current ripping left to right will dictate a different speed than a rocky shoreline at low tide with water depth of 3 to 5 feet. Still, the rule of thumb is to go as slow as you can to keep the eel in the strike zone and not become tangled in the structure you're fishing.

Whether you fish with conventional or spinning gear, after you cast keep the rod tip pointed almost straight above your head during the retrieve. This will create a bow in your line. When you feel that unmistakable bump, lower your tip, tighten the line, and then set the hook. This method works especially well with braided lines that have extreme sensitivity and almost no stretch.

LIVE WELLS

Round or oblong tanks are the choice for the serious live-bait anglers transporting bait. The goal is to minimize bait loss due to stress. Proper fish-handling procedures will result in surprisingly low mortality. It's amazing what chemically treated water with the proper oxygen will do!

When using fresh water for transporting herring, make sure the water hose is designed for human drinking water. Avoid using a common garden hose, which emits a foamy ingredient that keeps the rubber pliable but is poisonous to fish. Always run water through the hose first to flush out any sediment or impurities.

> **Tip**
> Sure Life brand foam-off removes harmful surface foam from your live well. Using this product will allow more oxygen to enter the water and prevent air starvation.

A pound of bait for 2 gallons of water is the general idea. It's best to hold and transport bait at lower water temperatures. This will reduce stress, and cold water holds more oxygen than warm. In addition, bait-fish consume less oxygen when they are cold. The oxygen consumption rate of fish at 80 degrees can be double the rate at 63 degrees. You can transport almost twice as many pounds of baitfish in the lower temperature with the same aeration system.

Everything you can do to keep the bait tanks clean will also help. Remove dead or dying fish immediately, and do not overcrowd your tank. The water in your live bait tank should not vary more than 4 degrees from the water in which your bait was taken, for the simple reason that shock will also kill them.

Live-Well Equipment

Incorrect aeration systems often cause unsatisfactory fish performance. When designing the air system, all of the following are important: Select round or oval bait wells. You should choose a powerful and a reliable air pump. When using mechanical aerators to produce oxygen, it's important to use air stones (diffusers) that produce medium to fine air bubbles.

The Sweetwater company makes the best air stones. These diffusers are machined from a solid block of glass-bonded silica. Dust and dirt particles will pass through. Diffusers with small bubbles will aerate 6.6 times as much water with the same amount of air.

Glass-bonded stones may require periodic cleaning when clogging occurs. When cleaning does become necessary because of bacterial buildup, a muriotic acid bath restores them to like-new performance. Be sure to rinse with fresh water before using.

> **Tip**
> Use two rubber O rings called diffusion bumpers on the air stone to elevate it off the bottom. This increases the surface area for bubble production.

Keep Alive oxygen infusers produce millions of microfine bubbles, increasing the surface area of the oxygen dissolved in water.

All this equipment will keep your bait alive, but that's not enough: Bait must also be kept calm. The stress of confinement can kill baitfish, so a product called Tranquil is available. Tranquil will calm fish and reduce injury during transportation. Other products like Shad Keeper will harden fish scales and protect the slime coating. Foam-off will remove harmful surface foam, allowing more oxygen to be dissolved in the water.

During hot weather, placing a sealed jug filled with frozen fresh water in the bait well will lower the water temperature and slow down the bait. Don't use too much, however; this can drop the water to an intolerable temperature and kill the fish. Oxygenated bait tanks should be treated with bait-saving chemicals to remove chlorine and contaminants. The tank should also be insulated with foam to maintain a more constant temperature during warm weather.

Live-Well Considerations for Boats

To a hard-core live-bait angler, the live well is the most important feature of a boat next to the engine and navigational equipment. Modern or custom installations boast powerful pumps and great circulation, water exchange volume, and outflow. The constant influx of fresh cool seawater keeps baits lively.

Check with some aftermarket custom builders before you settle on one setup. They have everything from fittings to multiple air compressors and stones. The new pure oxygen injection systems are great products as well. Many tournament anglers use this type of system.

If you have an older boat or one without a factory setup, a portable tank is the answer. These above-deck wells are simple to rig. As we noted above, round and oblong tanks offer by far the best, most sloshproof design. Avoid any tank design with square corners. For some reason, baits seem to press into any corner. Their bodies are touching each other, their gills are being pressed shut, and their noses are pressing on a hard surface. As competition intensifies, the fish begin to die.

Another important consideration is the tank's top seal. The tighter the seal, the better. This creates an area of air pressure in the tank similar to using a blender. With the top on, the fluid stays in; with a loose fit, it flies out.

You should also try to prevent turbulence within the tank. This can be accomplished by putting a nonskid mat called a waffle rubber between your tank and deck. These can be purchased at home improvement stores. They're designed for holding carpets in place on a hardwood floor. Double one over and put it under the entire tank; even in rough seas, this will keep the tank from sliding around.

More specifically, you can purchase a CoolerMat through catalogs and retailers. These mats are constructed of industrial-grade rubber and are designed to hold up in the harsh saltwater environment. It is a good idea to keep any mat on the clean side, because it'll quickly collect fish slime and dirt.

LIVE-BAIT TIPS

From a Jetty

Jetties are one of the best places to fish all types of live baits: herring, bunker, and eels. These man-made structures of rock are a haven for all sorts of marine life. Using bunker in these locations can create instant action.

Jetties around inlets offer the live-bait angler an added bonus. Because inlets have strong currents, they harbor various baitfish that feed on the plankton flow. Using live bunker in these situations will offer some exciting fishing. Be sure to carefully place the bait in the water rather than casting it, which can decrease its life dramatically. After placing the bait, walk along the jetty keeping it rather close; this is where most strikes will occur.

See part 1 for complete information on fishing jetties.

From a Boat

If you're fishing live eels from a boat, the sliding float rig is awesome. It's simple to construct. Use a 230-pound-test Spro TM barrel swivel and a 22-inch leader. We use a 5/0 Gamakatsu 024150 Octopus-style hook with a black finish.

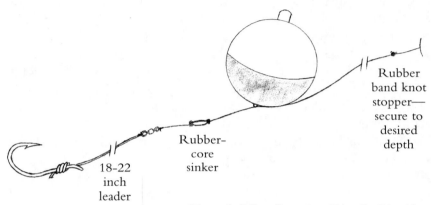

Rubber band knot stopper—secure to desired depth

Rubber-core sinker

18-22 inch leader

Live eel sliding float rig. *Brian R. Schneider*

With the depth recorder, find the depth you're fishing. Assuming the depth is about 12 feet, mark the main line about 2 feet short of that depth. Cut a rubber band in half and tie it with an overhand knot to the main line. Attach the float so it can slide between the knot and the rubber-core weight placed just above the swivel. This allows you to reel up the entire rig and the float will slide down to the weight.

Hook Setting

When to set the hook when livelining is one of the most often asked questions. Every expert an opinion on when and how to set the hook. Every type of fish has its own way of taking bait. Thus the type of tackle you're using and the fishing situations you're in will dictate the best technique.

Learning from others or from your own experimentation will help in the process. Simply put, what you want is for the fish to engulf the bait far enough down its gullet so that the hook is entirely inside its mouth. Watch your line or the fish itself. Make sure the fish feels no resistance from the line. Once the fish starts to swim away, you can set the hook.

15

Fishing with Artificials

Have you ever wondered what lies beneath the plastic of a guide's tackle locker? There are millions of lures on the market today—some great, some not so great. Taking a look into a professional guide's tackle box is like getting a hot stock tip from a Wall Street insider.

Just like flies, lures work best when they closely match the forage that the gamefish are feeding on. With artificials, presentation is the critical part of the fish-catching equation. You could spend an hour fishing next to an angler using the same plug—yet he's catching more fish than you. Is he retrieving the plug at a different speed? Or maybe casting and allowing the lure to swing while you're simply pulling it back through the current? Catch our drift? Just having the right plug, jig, or lure won't cut it. Presentation and selection should always be your first order of business.

While we can only speculate on what motivates a gamefish to strike an artificial lure, there are a few key factors that make one lure more productive than another. Running depth and speed are vital. Bluefish, for instance, respond well when a lure is working on or near the surface, while other species prefer a slow-moving bait near the bottom. If you don't get your lure near the strike zone, everything else becomes unimportant. Realism, size, color, and action are also crucial ingredients.

Let's take a look at the lures we prefer through the season.

PLUGS

Four- to 7-inch swimming plugs are among the deadliest lures to use when baits such as spearing, herring, sand eels, and rainfish are present. These minnow-shaped lures are now designed for fishing water depths that range from just subsurface to 10 feet, and most manufacturers are now making make them in both floating and sinking models. These lures have a built-in wiggle with a lifelike swimming action, and can be fished at slow or fast speeds. They're effective all season long.

The most popular types are the Bomber Long A series, the 5½- and 7-inch Redfin, Megabaits, and the Gags Grabbers Mambo Minnow series. The Yo-Zuri Crystal Minnow and Tsunami Long Stick also produce well in the shallow-swimming category. Because these lures are thin in diameter, they cast cast great and have produced strikes when all else has failed. Swimming plugs come in hundreds of colors, so pick a few and hold on tight.

Good trolling plugs when toothy bluefish are on the scene include the Predatek series of lures manufactured by Aussie Tackle (www.aussi-etackle.com). The company's Viper 150 series is manufactured with a unique enduroShok indestructible lip technology so the lip will not break. Vipers can be trolled to 6 knots without losing their realistic erratic movement in the water. They are available in 30 colors. Also check out the SandViper series, designed for skinny water and the surf.

Popping plugs are intended to work along the surface, making a disturbance with splashes that will attract all sorts of predatory fish. This type of plug is used exclusively during the day. There is a tremendous satisfaction in using poppers because of the ensuing strike is so visual. Stripers and bluefish love to crash poppers, although the two species tend to prefer different retrieves. Bluefish prefer a faster "ripping" motion across the water's surface, while stripers tend to go for more of a pop-and-stop motion.

Some of the most effective poppers that we use are the Creek Chub Striper Strike in the 1½- and 2-ounce sizes with a pearl white and blue flash finish; the Smack-It in either all-yellow or all-white; and the Gibbs Polaris in white with a red head. The great thing about poppers is that they can be cast long distances for bass and blues. This comes in particularly handy for surf anglers who need to reach feeding schools outside the normal casting range. The Gibbs pencil is a great popper for use in heavy surf conditions, and we will 9 out of 10 times go for an all-white lure. While wider-bodied poppers smack up and down, pencil poppers perform a side-to-side splashing sensation that drives fish absolutely wild.

Important lures for surf and jetty anglers include metal-lipped swimming plugs like the Gibbs Danny. This style of lure is a striped bass staple along the shores of the Northeast and swims on the surface with a vivid side-to-side motion that leaves a wake when retrieved slowly. Metal-lipped swimmers are large wooden plugs generally used during the fall mullet and bunker run—but don't write them off for spring months, when large pods of herring and bunker are migrating through your local waters. It's a well-known fact that large fish like to eat big bait because they expend less energy to get the same amount of food. With their side-to-side movement, metal-lipped swimmers closely resemble lumbering injured bait and will elicit a natural predatory response.

Over the last few years, people have discovered the effectiveness of handcrafted wooden swimmers that are totally sealed with epoxy. They're available in a wide variety of colors and sold at local tackle shops and the fishing flea markets held during winter months. Custom handmade swimmers are available from Bass Wood Lures, Cannon Lures, TB Lures, and the coveted Lefties. These lures are not easy to come by, and there are days in the surf when having these custom-made plugs is like having gold.

> ### Tip
> Change a plug's hardware to heavy-duty split rings and 4X trebles to ensure that when the big fish hits, your hardware won't fail.

You can alter the action of these plugs by bending the lip. Bend it down and the plug will run near the surface, depending on how far it's bent; bend it up and the plug will run deeper. Make sure the lip remains perfectly level, whether bent up or down. An inaccurate bend will cause a wrong presentation and could elicit a refusal.

Metal-lipped swimmers can also be altered by increasing the size of the front treble hook. We do this because bass usually attack the eyes of prey, making it useful to have a strong hook in front. Also, remove the tail treble and replace with a hook shank covered with bucktail; then cut off the bend of the hook so only the shank is left. This will add a tantalizing action to these swimmers, which can at times make the difference between a hit and a refusal.

In addition to metal-lipped swimmers, we also will use wooden-lipped swimmers such as the Gibbs Casting Swimmer—better known the bottle plug. This plug's all-wood construction includes a concave wooden lip that digs into the water. This feature make it an excellent choice for rough surf conditions and rips during both day and night. Most popular is the 3-ounce size in all-white or all-yellow.

Blown foam plastic plugs like the Atom 40 and Atom Jr. are also favorites in the metal-lipped swimmer category. Atoms have a lazy side-to-side swimming action that huge fish cannot resist, which is how they've earned their reputation for catching fish over 40 pounds.

Needlefish lures work all season when sand eels are in our waters. They run from 5 to 7 inches long and ½ to 2 ounces in weight, and are easy to cast. We prefer to use the Boone, Habbs, and Gibbs in a variety of colors, including olive over white, blue over white, and all-black for night applications.

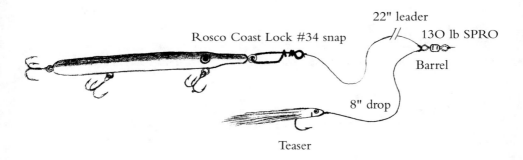

Needlefish with teaser rig. *Brian R. Schneider*

Because needlefish plugs feature built-in action, it's important to fish them with a *slow* deliberate retrieve, with its action controlled by the tip of the rod. We like to make this plug dart from side to side by twitching the rod tip. It takes some discipline and practice to get this technique right, but once you've mastered it, it'll become one of your favorite ways to catch fish.

METALS AND TINS

When fish are feeding far from the shoreline, casting metals is sometimes your only option. These chrome-colored lures are available in multiple sizes and weights. Although they don't really resemble anything that swims, they're great producers because of their shiny appearance.

The size and weight of a metal will dictate its swimming motion. Both should be increased in rough water. We like to remove the treble hook and replace it with a single hook dressed with bucktail or feathers for added action. Our favorite metal styles are the Crippled Herring, Acme Kastmaster, Hopkins, and Deadly Dick. Most anglers reserve their metals for bluefish, but we've found that they can be equally productive for stripers and particularly little tuna species, like false albacore and bonito.

Prior to World War II, tin squids were the standard weapons of surf anglers, and they're still used today to imitate sand eels and large spearing. These legendary lures perfectly to simulate the small, slender baitfish.

Probably the most popular metal lure today is the Ava-style diamond jig, which resembles a sand eel. The casting version of this lure is dressed with a surgical tail and is available in a wide variety of tube colors. On a boat, we generally prefer tailless jigs dressed with a single hook, which we drop directly to the bottom and jig with a straight up-and-down motion to resemble a fleeing sand eel.

SOFT BAITS

Soft plastic lures have been a staple Florida bait for many years among anglers targeting sea trout, redfish, snook, and other gamefish. Over the past decade, soft baits have moved their way up to the Northeast Coast, taking the scene by storm. With new styles and colors popping up every fishing season, soft baits continue to gain popularity for one simple reason: They catch fish. Any fish that eats lures will eat a jig dressed with a soft plastic body. The key factor is selecting the rubber that most directly imitates your native baitfish.

Lunker City Fin-S fish revolutionized soft baits. These thin-bodied artificials have an erratic action that will draw instinctive strikes from all types of gamefish. With their long, slender bodies, they're best fished when spearing, grass shrimp, and rainfish are present. Look to match local baitfish size, shape, and profile when making your selection. Soft baits have tremendous versatility when matched with the various lead-head sizes out on the market today and can be used successfully in all tidal waters from the beach, jetty, or boat.

When trying to imitate larger baits like mullet, herring, and bunker, it's tough to beat the Sassy Shad style of soft baits. These baits can be cast from the surf, jetty, or boat and retrieved in at mid- to deep depths; they can also be jigged from boats off the bottom with an up-

and-down motion. They're deadly when trolled with wire line on umbrella rigs that hold multiple hooked shad bodies. We add a 1- to 2-ounce painted jighead that matches the color of the shad body. This weighted head, coupled with its constantly moving paddle tail, creates a very realistic look.

> **Tip**
> When rigging Sassy Shads to jigheads, cut the shad body's head to match the size and shape of the jighead. Use a nail glue or superglue to produce a custom fit.

Just when we thought the industry had hit the ceiling with soft bait design, someone said, "Why don't we put the lead *inside* the rubber body and use multiple colors on each lure?" Today's new soft plastics represent almost any baitfish. Their colors and action are so exact, they look as if you should keep them in your live well. Running 3 to 9 inches long, they sport a new holographic foil finish and realistic detail to match the natural characteristics of the native forage. We've caught fish on pretty much all the color selections out there, though bunker, pearl, and chartreuse seem to be the top producers.

Soft baits can be fished in deep or shallow water, but we generally concentrate on the lower half of the water column. After making a cast, let the softie settle, keep your rod tip straight out, and lift the tip without cranking to make the jig work. Then take a few cranks and repeat. As always, presentation is key. A slow-falling wobble will tempt even the most finicky fish. You can also bounce plastic bait off the bottom to mimic an injured baitfish. A steady, slow retrieve can be deadly, too, particularly when fishing from a drifting boat.

In fast or heavy current, soft baits have action all by themselves, without your moving at all. We recommend soft baits with a thinner, deeper profile and a forked tail, which have a realistic natural wiggle. In slower current, you may want to enhance the action by twitching (not jerking) the rod tip. Repeat this every few seconds, and do not be over-anxious. This causes the bait to change direction. Probably the biggest mistake anglers make when fishing soft baits is to cast and retrieve as fast as possible.

SECRETS OF THE EEL SKIN PLUG REVEALED!

One of the earliest striper lures along the Northeast Coast was a cedar jig often covered with eel skin. During the late 1800s, Buzzards Bay anglers used these lethal jigs to catch many monster bass over 50 pounds. Our first experience with eel skin plugs was in the late 1960s, fishing the Eighth Avenue Jetty in Belmar, New Jersey. Shell E. watched an angler catch striped bass after striped bass using a lure he'd never seen before, amazed at the lure's lifelike action. Finally, he had to ask the angler what he was using and where he could get one. He was told you have to make them.

Seeing Shell's interest, the angler walked him through each step in building his own. This would be one of the most fascinating lures Shell E. would ever use. The eel skin plug is most suitable for beach and jetty fishing. In the early days, we would put them over metal-lipped swimming plugs and subsurface plugs. These were wooden plugs, so to keep the skins from rotting we put them in kosher salt solution. Today we generally put skins on the Atom Jr. plug. With this plastic lure, the skin can be kept in the freezer between trips so it doesn't dry out.

Eel skin lures are generally fished at night, though in the right conditions we have also had tremendous success in daylight. Reel the plug in slowly at night to allow it to swim in the current.

One of the key advantages of the eel skin plug is its ability to adapt to different situations. By bending the lip, you can alter the action of the

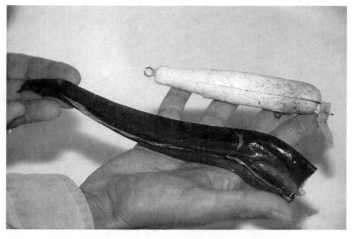

Veteran anglers know the importance of eelskin plugs. Use them on metal-lip swimmers like Danny plugs and Atom Jr's. They take trophy bass every season. Caris

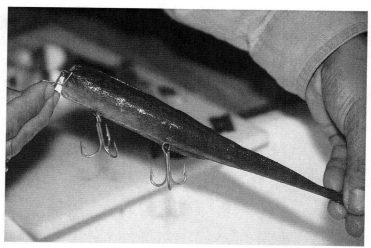

The finished product. Caris

plug to suit your needs. Just like any other metal-lipped swimmer, by bending the lip down the plug will work at or near the surface, depending on how far the lip is bent. By bending the lip up, the plug dives. Another trick when the eel is skinned is to turn it inside out. This gives the plug a light blue color that's more like a natural baitfish than an eel.

Eels can be purchased at fish markets or caught by potting (discussed in chapter 14). For us, skinning eels and customizing new plugs that come on this market has been part of the fun. It may seem like a lot of work, but it's really quite simple, and their effectiveness is well worth the time and effort.

The easiest way to skin an eel is to nail its head behind the gills then peel the skin toward the tail with a pair of pliers. Eel skins can be put in a kosher salt brine, an age-old technique that has yet to be improved on. You can also just freeze them.

Step by Step with an Atom Jr. Swimmer

1. Choose an eel about the same diameter as the plug and long enough for its tail to extend beyond the plug.
2. Remove all plug hooks, then slide the eel skin up the plug's body. Make sure you are careful near the hook, mounting barrel swivels so as to not break the skin.
3. Work the eel skin up to the plate, making sure it has a snug fit.

4. Secure the head area with 50-pound braided Dacron, making a series of overhand knots.

5. Trim the tag ends, and melt with a flame. Secure the knot with head cement.

6. Trim the excess eel skin. This will make the plug uniform, preventing any distortions in its action.

7. Use a single-edged razor to cut the skin by the barrel swivel.

8. Insert an open-eye treble hook through the barrel swivel.

9. Close the open-eye treble hook with pliers.

10. The finished product: the most realistic plug you could ever use.

Fishing a Rigged Eel

The rigged eel has been the secret weapon of the die-hard striped bass angler for more than 100 years. Eel squids come in various sizes and weights, which will determine how high or deep the eel will ride in the water column. The best eel squids are made from pure block tin. You can control a squid's action by bending it to a greater or lesser degree, as conditions will dictate. When considering which size eel squid to use in a particular situation, keep in mind that weight is only one factor. The overall design, the wing-to-eel ratio, and the speed of retrieve are much more important in determining how the eel rides on the water than weight. The best way to give the eel its natural S-like swimming motion is to simply raise and lower the rod tip during your retrieve. Crawling or bouncing along the bottom can be quite effective and can encourage

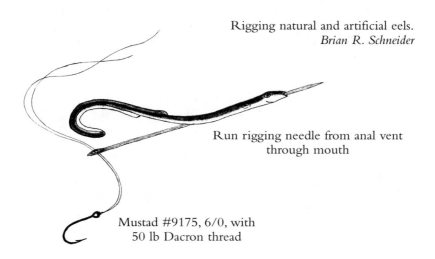

Rigging natural and artificial eels.
Brian R. Schneider

Run rigging needle from anal vent through mouth

Mustad #9175, 6/0, with 50 lb Dacron thread

violent strikes. You can also give your plug the snakelike motion of a natural swimming eel simply by bending it.

Natural dead rigged eels are generally fished at night, while the artificial rubber rigged eels have become very popular during daylight hours when sand eels are abundant. One excellent artificial eel is the 8-inch FelmLee eel in natural olive. Success with rigged eels comes with practice. Once this method is mastered, it will be a potent weapon for taking large striped bass.

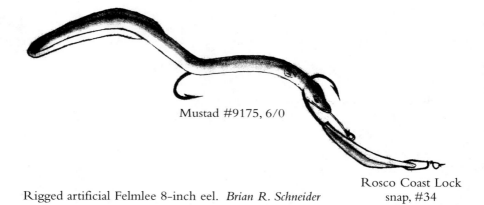

Mustad #9175, 6/0

Rigged artificial Felmlee 8-inch eel. *Brian R. Schneider*

Rosco Coast Lock
snap, #34

LOADING PLUGS

Wind is always a factor when fishing the surf, and somehow the best action seems to occur on days when the wind is howling off the ocean. Working lightweight plastic swimmers like Redfins, Bombers, Megabaits, and some of the newest Yo-Zuri and Tsunami swimmers can be a problem if you're casting into the wind.

The solution is to increase the weight of the lure simply by adding fluid to the body chamber. A great plug to load is the Cotton Cordell Redfin Series. We have had tremendous success over the years using

> ### Tip
> When sand eels are the predominant bait in heavy surf, use a loaded plastic Super Strike Needle Fish.

these quality swimmers. We've also learned, through the process of elimination, that the fluid of choice is mineral oil. Water has a tendency to evaporate over time, while bunker oil is messy and smelly. Mineral oil, however, will not alter a plug's buoyancy or action. In addition, it prevents tumbling when weighted properly.

Loading plastic swimmers is simple. You will need:
- A rigging needle
- A syringe or similar tool
- Mineral oil
- A knife
- Epoxy glue

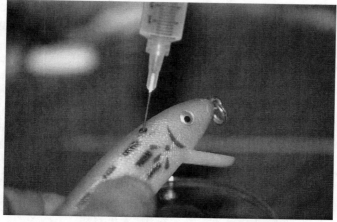

Loading plastic swimmers can improve the lures' effectiveness. Use 5cc of mineral oil for small lures and 7cc for large ones. Caris

1. Heat the rigging needle red hot. Then penetrate the plug just off the center seam. This keeps the plug from splitting and leaking. At first you may be tempted to use a small drill bit, but that's a mistake. The drill bit will make a cleaner hole and will be tougher to close. Using a rigging needle will make a small mushroom-rimmed hole. This plastic will be used later.
2. Use a syringe to inject the fluid into the hollow chamber of the plug. As a rule, fill 7-inch plugs with 7 ccs of fluid, and 5-inch plugs with 5 ccs. Plastic swimmers vary in shape and size, so experiment with the amount of fluid. If the chamber is overfilled, you may ruin the action. Also, using too little will make the lure less effective.

3. Once the plug is loaded, heat the knife point and use it to smooth over the mushroom, clogging the hole.
4. For added protection, use a two-part epoxy glue to cover the pierced area.

BRAIDED FISHING LINES

One of the questions our clients ask us most often is whether they should use braided line. Simply put, braided lines have become our lines of choice for all spin- and conventional-fishing stuations. With a little understanding and experience, using these lines will give any saltwater angler a decisive edge from the first cast.

The first-generation superlines were made with abrasive fibers that cut rod guides and ruined expensive equipment. Technology has improved, however, and lines today are rounder and more compact. They will not bury in the spool. Superbraids are smooth and ultrastrong. Because they are designed with no stretch and very thin diameters, these lines will outperform monofilament in almost any fishing situation.

Superbraids are structurally superior to other lines. They have unbelievable pound-test strength to size ratio. For example, 50-pound braid is approximately equivalent to 12-pound mono. Casting distance increases with the smaller diameter, and these lines have no reel memory.

> **Tip**
> Braided lines make excellent fly backing, adding capacity and strength but also featuring less drag in the water. Stren and PowerPro make a hi-vis yellow line that's easily visible.

Braids are hassle-free in any weather conditions and will not deteriorate as fast as mono. In addition, their smaller diameter means you can fit more on your reel.

Spooling with Braids

Braids have different characteristics than monofilament. Therefore, remember to leave about 10 to 15 yards of monofilament on the spool before you begin spooling with braided line. This will eliminate the chance that your braided line will slide around the barrel.

The best knot to use when attaching the monofilament backing to the braid is the uni-to-uni line splice. This knot is simple to tie and will make for an ultraclear transition. When spooling your spinning reels, keep the spool on a roller system, similar to what you'd find on household paper towels. It's important not to overspool your reels. We recommend leaving approximately ⅛ inch below the rim of the reel; you won't sacrifice any distance, but you'll eliminate the wind knots that can result from overspooling.

In our years of saltwater fishing, we have seen many changes in fishing tackle. The introduction of new reels and especially graphite rods has changed the way we fish. Being able to feel every action of the live bait or artificial lure is the key. The extra sensitivity of braids enables us to set the hook at the first indication of a fish striking.

Braided lines are remarkably strong, and with their near-zero stretch, hookset is a snap. Your main concern is not to overreact. Too strong a motion may pull the hook free. Remember, because there is no stretch, every inch your rod tip moves will equal an inch of movement of your bait or lure.

A WORD ON SPINNING AND CONVENTIONAL RODS

We would be remiss if we didn't mention rods in this chapter, simply because the rod is such a critical tool. Rods are to fishermen as ropes are to rock climbers. Simply put, you cannot be successful without the right stick. There is an old saying out there: "Never bring a knife to a gunfight." Similarly, you wouldn't want to show up for a major striper blitz in screaming winds and pounding surf with a 7-foot ultralight. Nor would you go seeking weakfish with an 11-foot surf stick.

While there are many good rod manufacturers today, we feel that one in particular has the best rods for any saltwater fishing situation. The St. Croix Rod Company has been building rods in Park Falls, Wisconsin, longer than most of us have been alive. It offers saltwater (and freshwater) anglers high-quality rods and a reasonable price. Whether you want to spend less than $100 or more than $400, St. Croix has a rod for you. Fishing rod design is improving dramatically, and St. Croix is on the cutting edge of this technology. Today anglers are using lighter, stronger, and faster blanks for all saltwater fishing applications.

The following table gives a sampling of the rods we choose in specific situations.

Shore Catch Guide Service Rod Chart

Application	St. Croix Rod Description	Line Rating	Species
Light Boat Spin	Avid 7'6" Medium Fast Action	8–15 #	Small to Midsized Stripers & Blues
	Avid 7'0" Medium Heavy Fast Action	10–17 #	Weakfish
	Premier Surf 7'0" Moderate Fast Light Action	4–8 #	Casting Small Plugs, Poppers, Metal,
	Tidemaster 7'6" Medium Fast Action	8–17 #	& Soft Baits
	Tidemaster 6'6" Medium Heavy Fast Action	10–20 #	Back Bay Fishing
Heavy Boat Spin	Tidemaster 8'0" Heavy Fast Action	12–25 #	Large Stripers & Blues
	Tidemaster 8'0" Extra Heavy Extra Fast Action	15–40 #	Casting Large Plugs, Poppers,
	Tidemaster 7'0" Heavy Fast Action	12–25 #	& Heavier Metals
			Large Sassy Shads
Light Boat Conventional	Tidemaster 7'0" Medium Fast	8–17 #	Small to Midsized Stripers & Blues
	Tidemaster 7'3" Medium Moderate	8–17 #	Weakfish
	Premier 7'0" Medium Fast	10–17 #	Light Deep-Water Jigging
	Avid 7'0" Medium Heavy Extra Fast	10–17 #	Casting/Jigging Small Soft Baits
	Legend Elite 7'6" Medium Heavy Fast	12–25 #	Back Bay Fishing
Heavy Boat Conventional	Avid 7'6" Medium Heavy Fast	20–50 #	Large Stripers & Blues
	Avid 8'0" Heavy Fast	20–50 #	Livelining Large Baits
	Premier 7'6" Medium Heavy Fast	17–40 #	Heavy Deep-Water Jigging
	Premier 6'9" Heavy Fast	20–50 #	Casting Large Plugs and Sassy Shads
Bluewater Boat	Premier 6'0" Medium Fast	15–30 #	Trolling, Chunking, Jigging
	Premier 6'6" Medium Heavy Fast	20–40#	False Albacore, Skipjack, Bonito
	Premier 6'0" Heavy Fast—Slick Butt	30–50#	Bluefin & Yellowfin Tuna
	Premier 6'6" Heavy—Slick Butt	30–50#	Marlin, Sharks
Wire-Line Trolling Boat	Premier 8'0" Medium Heavy Fast—Slick Butt	20–50#	Large Stripers Wire-Line Trolling
Light Surf Wading Spin	Premier Surf 7'0" Medium Light	6–10 #	Small to Midsized Stripers & Blues
	Premier Surf 8'0" Medium	6–17 #	Weakfish
	Avid Surf 8'0" Medium	6–17 #	Calm Surf & Jetty Fishing Back Bay Wading
Heavy Surf Jetty Spin	Premier Surf 8'6" Medium Moderate Fast	6–17 #	Large Stripers & Blues
	Avid 9'0" Surf Medium Moderate Fast	6–20 #	Strong Surf & Jetty Fishing
	Premier Surf 10 Medium Moderate Fast	8–20 #	Casting Large Plugs, Baits, Metals
	Avid 10'0" Medium Heavy Moderate Fast	10–25 #	
Surf & Jetty Conventional	Premier Surf 8'6" Medium Moderate Fast	6–17 #	Casting Plugs, Poppers, Jigs
	Premier Surf 10'6" Medium Heavy	10–25 #	Livelining & Cut-Bait Fishing
	Avid 10'0" Medium Moderate Fast	10–25 #	
	Avid 11'0" Heavy Moderate Fast	15–50 #	

16

The Night Game

Fishing at night is unheard of for many anglers, while for others it has become second nature. In many areas, you'll find close-knit fraternities of fishermen who live under the cover of darkness and come alive at night like an old Lon Chaney movie.

And rightly so. Nighttime fishing does have its advantages.

Striped bass and weakfish, for instance, are nocturnal; darkness puts them on the prowl and will outproduce the daytime even if you invest an equal number of hours. Many times these fish will be right at your feet at night.

Night time is the right time for trophy bass. Capt. Jim displays a 25-pounder that hit a Chuck Furimsky sand eel. Freda

In addition, nights are generally calmer and less windy than during the day—if there's any wind at all. There are fewer crowds, fewer boats, and no Jet Skis to deal with. And then there is the ambience of being bathed with darkness rather than with sunlight.

You'll also find that feeding fish move much closer to the beach at night than during the day. In the cover of darkness, they feel comfortable in shallow waters that they might avoid during the day. At night, fish will come over sandbars to invade a flat, or even prowl the trough created from waves breaking along the shoreline.

WHEN TO GO

The most productive time of year for venturing out at night is from late spring through mid- to late fall. Early spring isn't as productive as other times of the year, because colder water temperatures slow feeding activities. Striped bass and weakfish are still trying to acclimate to this from the passing winter.

Summer is usually one of the most productive seasons for nighttime fishing. On hot summer days, conditions such as increasing water temperatures and a sun that is high in the sky can often produce what anglers refer to as the summer doldrums. This is basically a period of feeding inactivity in the waters close to a beach or back bay. As a result, nighttime is when you'll find the bass and weakfish feeding.

In fall when blitzes are common during the day, fish can and often do turn on again at some time during the night. You may not have all the surface commotion you saw several hours earlier, but fish will still feed high in the water column. Bass in particular won't have any problem taking an artificial fished slowly across the surface.

FINE-TUNE YOUR SENSES

Fishing at night is definitely going to be more of a challenge than during the day. Still, your mission can be simplified and approached with confidence if you develop a nighttime awareness that puts you in touch with your surroundings. Visual clues and sensations are of course greatly minimized at night; you won't be able to see many of the daytime indicators that you use to locate fish.

It will be to your advantage to fish locales whose topography you're familiar with. If you know where to find fish-attracting structural features—sandbars, drop-offs, cuts, and rips—it is a good bet that you'll find fish present along these same structures at night. Use them as a starting point for your fishing.

Developing a good sense of night vision will be important not only to your success at night but also to your personal safety. In any densely populated areas that you fish, there will be diffuse light present that you can use to your advantage. This light will come from surrounding structures, such as boardwalks, bridges, roadways, or homes. Moonlight can also be helpful.

> **Tip**
> It's a good idea to carry a compass with you when wading out into back bay areas. A compass will point you in the right direction if fog rolls in quickly and you can't see any lights from the land.

With practice you can train your eyes to use diffuse light. If you're wading in a back bay or fishing on a jetty, for example, you can turn and face any available streetlight while tying a knot. This allows the streetlight to reflect off your monofilament or fluorocarbon. You won't need to turn on a light that could spook any fish close by.

You'll also need a good head or neck lamp to provide light when out there in the night game. As an alternative, you can carry a small handheld flashlight that will easily fit inside your waders. One of the advantages of holding a flashlight in your hand is that you can put more direct light closer to your feet, making it easier to see where you're stepping. The disadvantage is that it ties up a free hand.

It's also a good idea to carry a small light with you as a backup just in case your main light breaks, gets lost, or just doesn't work properly. This doesn't have to be anything big; a mini light will do. Make sure you check the illumination of your lights the night before you go out. Performing this check during the day won't give you a true idea of a bulb's brightness. Replace the batteries if necessary. Don't pinch your pennies here.

Relying on your other senses to tune in to your surroundings is also critical to your success at night. Your senses of sound, feel, and even smell should become fine-tuned. Feel during casting and retrieving is critical, allowing you to recognize where your artificial lands and what it's doing in the water.

Hearing is an important tool that will work to your advantage at night. As you approach a location, actually listen for fish. Any thrashing, popping, or slurping that you might hear around you will indicate that fish are feeding in the area. On calm nights, particularly during summer, these sounds can be very distinct. On rough or windy nights, however, your listening will be impeded.

A prime example of this is when striped bass are feeding on grass shrimp or sand eels in back bay waters. These baits move at or near the surface, and you'll hear a distinctive sound when stripers inhale them along with a pocket of air. When they're being sipped from the surface, a slightly different sound will be audible. With experience, you'll learn to identify what species of bait and fish may be present simply by the sounds you hear.

Many savvy night owls have also developed an acute sense of smell that they use to their advantage. Some baits, such as Atlantic menhaden, have a characteristic smell that you can pick up on. We can all remember times when we've said, "Boy, it even smells fishy."

A sense of feel will take you a long way, too. With spinning or conventional tackle, work to develop a feel for how far your cast is going based on how long it takes your line to go limp after you cast. With a fly rod, distance is of course easier to determine based on how much line shoots out of your basket.

Once you start your retrieve, having a good sense of the tension in your line can help you determine how far your artificial is from you. This feeling will change as the drag on your line decreases while the articial gets closer. You could also keep track of the number of cranks you take on your reel or strips on your fly line. Always knowing where your artificial is in relationship to your position is important. This is particularly true when fishing a jetty at night so you don't pull your offering into the rocks.

You can also learn to detect whether your plug or fly is tracking properly through the water. Any small seaweed or detritus that gets snagged on your hook should be recognized and felt as you retrieve. If it isn't, you can end of with many wasted casts and retrieves. For the same reason, it's a good idea to always check your artificial for any signs detritus before you cast again. Doing this will definitely slow your fishing down, but it's still a good habit to get into. Just about all that you do at night will be slower anyway, including your retrieve, so one more thing shouldn't be a problem.

NIGHT FISHING STRATEGIES

Approach any waters that you are going to fish in a stealthy manner. If you're on foot, cast first from the beach into the waters that you might be planning to wade into. At night, fish are more likely to be holding right at your feet; by all means avoid spooking them.

Big stripers start to feed right at dusk. Shore Catch fly fisher Jim Ardito displays a beauty. Quigley

Some of the most exciting moments of nighttime fishing can occur when fishing a topwater artificial on a calm night. Here an artificial slowly worked across the surface will produce a trailing wake that will entice many fish to strike violently. Many times the water will explode just a few feet in front of you as the strike is made.

We don't recommend using sinking lines along jetties at night, because these lines can easily become entangled in the rocks that protrude in front of you. Once this happens, trying to climb down to untangle the line will put you in a high-risk situation. You can, however, use sinking line in back bays along ledges and drop-offs where there are minimal obstructions.

If you're fly casting at night, there are several factors to watch out for. If you learned to cast while looking at your backcast, you have a problem. You'll need to work on *feeling* the rod load instead. Practice this during the day without looking back. If this doesn't work for you, your other alternative is to experiment with the new glow-in-the-dark fly lines. This new technology will allow you to see where your line is.

In addition, you need to always be cognizant of where your back-cast is going. In the dark, many fly fishers tend to drop the rod tip on the backcast. This will result in beating your flies against an upwardly sloping berm or jetty rocks behind you. Keep your tip up. Remember, where your tip is pointed is where your line and fly will go.

Also, make sure that no one is walking behind you before you begin your cast. Many times it's difficult for an angler who decides to walk behind you to even recognize that you're fly fishing. It's your responsibility to make sure that all is clear.

BOATING AT NIGHT

If you are venturing out with your boat at night, be extremely cautious. We recommend only fishing areas that you are totally familiar with; never attempt to fish new waters at night. Doing so runs the risk of running into submerged objects such as pilings or other obstructions that are uncharted. It's not worth risking hull or prop damage to be an explorer.

> *Tip*
> Ameripack (www.ameripack.com) makes a great water-proof mini light with a high-intensity bulb that can be clipped to your jacket, hat, or surf bag. It's great for giving you a focused beam when you need to tie any knots, but it also throws enough light to be used as your primary source if you like. Carrying two lights only adds to your safety.

Besides your USCG-approved safety equipment (discussed in chapter 8), your boat should be equipped with a GPS/chart plotter that you are thoroughly familiar with. At night, this is your eyes. It will locate any channel markers, buoys, or other charted navigational aids within several yards of their exact location. Having preprogrammed routes entered into your chart plotter will also work to your advantage, because you'll know beforehand where you're going and what's in front of you.

You should realize, however, that GPS is not completely error-proof, and sometimes a discrepancy of only a few yards can make the

> **Tip**
> If you're wading out into a bay and need to leave your gear behind you on the beach, use a small cyalume nightstick to mark the location of your personal belongings. These nightsticks will glow for several hours and are visible for a good distance.

difference between having and avoiding a collision. For this reason, you should use a spotlight in conjunction with your GPS to locate what you're seeing on your chart. This could be a handheld spotlight or one that's permanently mounted on your boat. Aim the spotlight in the direction that your chart is marking the obstacle and look for the light bouncing off the reflective materials found on these objects. You will now be able to sight the exact location of the object. One caution: Make sure you don't shine the light on any boats in the vicinity. This would be similar to having a flashlight shined in your face while in a dark room. Doing so will have a tendency to blind the operator of the other boat momentarily.

Radar offers another advantage by revealing any uncharted obstacles in your path. Most importantly, this includes other boats that might pose an immediate collision danger.

Despite all your electronics and experience, however, you still always run the risk of hitting floating lumber or other debris that just isn't visible at night. This should always be on your mind. Taking for granted that your path is unobstructed can get you into trouble. For this reason, running hard from location to location like you might do during the daytime is not advisable. Cut down your speed to reduce any damage that may occur if an unfortunate collision with any floating object does takes place.

Not every angler can fish the prime night hours and still make it to work the next day. It's definitely hard to do. You should, however, try to experience this productive time at some point during the season. We think you will be surprised at how active the "nightlife" really is.

17

Fly Fishing the Guide's Way

Throughout this book, you have read many of our tactics and techniques for saltwater fly fishing. For us and many other anglers, fly fishing is our favorite way of catching fish in salt water. No other fishing method offers as much challenge and freedom. Many consider fly fishing an art form. We at Shore Catch look at all methods of fishing as art forms; some are just a bit more technical than others. In our minds, however, fly fishing is the essence of the sport.

Fighting fish on the fly from the surf. Quigley

Many anglers tell us that they always bring a fly rod along in case an opportunity presents itself—meaning, when *they* feel fish will hit a fly. In our minds and hearts, there is never a time when fly fishing is not an applicable method for catching fish. Sure, there may be times when other methods will outfish the fly rod, but there are also times when the fly rod undoubtedly outdoes every other method.

We've heard a lot of misconceptions about fly fishing, including:
- "The fish are too deep, my fly will never be able to get down there."
- "The bait is too big, I'll never be able to imitate that with a fly."
- "The wind is too strong; no one could cast in this stuff."

These are all plausible objections, but they certainly don't prevent us from catching fish in salt water on the fly every day that we go out.

There are many obstacles that challenge fly fishers every day on the water. Beginners seem to always struggle with the cast. There's only one way of overcoming this obstacle, and that is practice. Casting is the core of fly fishing; the better you can cast, the more fish you will catch, period. We have heard many say that you don't have to be a good caster to catch fish on the fly in salt water. Yes, you can and certainly will catch some fish if you're a marginal caster, but the fact remains that better casters will catch more fish in all situations. We encourage you to continuously improve on your casting. Take lessons; observe others who have mastered the cast; and, most importantly, practice.

In this chapter we will discuss some of the biggest challenges that saltwater fly fishers face day in and day out: fly selection, line selections for deep-water fly fishing, fly fishing in strong winds, and line control.

FLY SELECTION

Fly selection in salt water can be just as important as in fresh water. Our northeastern gamefish—stripers, blues, weakfish, little tuna, and large tuna—can all become very selective feeders. Matching the prevalent baits in overall size, profile, and length will be to your advantage 90 percent of the time. (The other 10 percent of the time, just the opposite holds true: There's so much bait that the fish will choose a fly because it stands out. A striper, for instance, might pick out a large, bright fly—a yellow or chartreuse Lefty's Deceiver, say—and strike out at it because it's different from the pack. These unusual times can be great learning experiences for fly anglers.)

A good fly fisher always understands the bait—from its prevalence to its size, profile, color, and swimming pattern. All these factors play an important role in selecting a fly or flies for the day. You don't want to throw a slender, translucent spearing pattern when large-profiled mullet are around. Rather, you'd look for a fly with more of a three-dimensional round body shape that would swim or wake just below the water's surface.

In addition, color can play a crucial role when choosing a fly. We have never seen an all-chartreuse or pink baitfish. So why do these colors consistently produce? Some say that baitfish carry hues of these colors in them. Others claim that bright colors will work better than natural colors when the water is off color, or during bright days. We feel that all these arguments have merit at times, but the best way to figure it out for yourself is to carry a variety of colors and experiment when one color isn't working. For instance, if you're fishing an olive-and-white Surf Candy during the spearing run, and the fish are not responding to it, change over to a brighter chartreuse or yellow fly of the same pattern.

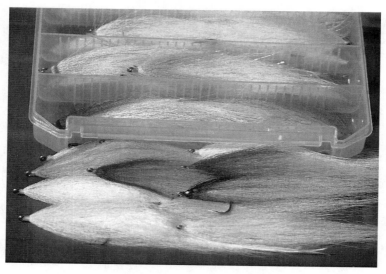

Long bright flies, like these bucktail deceivers from Bob Popovics, are great choices when trying to imitate large baits. Quigley

The Guide's Fly Box

All that said, we bring you a serious look into the Shore Catch fly box. There are many effective saltwater patterns tied by many talented saltwater fly tiers out there. Living on the Jersey Shore, we have had the opportunity to fish with one of the industry's most noted saltwater fly designers, Bob Popovics. Over the last 30 years, Bob has developed a series of effective, durable, and realistic flies called PopFleyes. We do use flies from other designers from time to time, yet we remain disposed toward the PopFleyes patterns because they so closely emulate the baits that we try to match here in the Northeast.

Bob's approach to tying offers simplicity of construction, for both easy tying and effective fishing. Bob's innovative introduction of epoxy and silicone in flies during the 1970s changed the path of fly design 180 degrees, and today we thank him for giving us such wonderful flies to fish.

Bait	Attributes	Pattern	Fly Designer	Colors
Spearing	1–6" Slender Bait	Surf Candy	Bob Popovics	Olive/White, Yellow
	Olive Greenish Back	Jiggy Fly	Bob Popovics	Chartreuse/White
	Pearl Belly	Clouser Minnow	Bob Clouser	White, Black (night)
	Silver Center Stripe	Mushmouth	Dave Skok	
	Translucent	Sparse Lefty's Deceiver	Lefty Kreh	
		Simpleclone	Bob Popovics	
Sand Eel	½–8" Bait	Jiggy Fly	Bob Popovics	Yellow, Blue/White
	Greenish Brown Back	Stick Candy	Bob Popovics	Chartreuse/White
	Pearl Underside	Keel Eel	Bob Popovics	Red, Black (Night)
	Long and Slender (Straight)	Foam Slider	Eric Peterson	All-White
	Small Eye			
	Pointy Nose			
Rainfish	1–3" Slender Bait	Surf Candy	Bob Popovics	Tan/White, All-White,
(Bay Anchovy)	Tan Back	Deep Candy	Bob Popovics	Chartreuse/White
	Pearly Belly	Jiggy Fly	Bob Popovics	
	Large Eye	Mushmouth	Dave Skok	
	Stout Nose	Clouser Minnow	Bob Clouser	
	Silver Center Stripe			
	Translucent			
Herring	6–14" Bait	Hollow Fleye	Bob Popovics	Blue/White, Green/White,
	Large Profile	Bucktail Deceiver	Bob Popovics	Red Head/White Body
	Greenish Blue Back	Lefty's Deceiver	Lefty Kreh	All-White
	Silver/Pearl Belly	Mega Mushy	Dave Skok	Chartreuse/White
	Slender Body	Half-and-Half	Clouser/Kreh	

(continued)

Bait	Attributes	Pattern	Fly Designer	Colors
Large Menhaden (Bunker)	8–14" Bait Very Large Profile Round Head Greenish Brown Back Hues of Pink/Yellow Pearl Belly Black Spots on Belly	Dino's Bunker Fly Cotton Candy Large Lefty's Deceivers	Dino Torino Bob Popovics Lefty Kreh	Tan, Yellow, Pink, White, Yellow/White All-White All-Chartreuse
Small Menhaden (Peanut Bunker)	2–6" Bait Large Profile Blue/Purple/Goldish Back Pearl Silver Belly Black Spots on Belly	Bucktail Bunker Lefty's Deceiver Baby Angel Half-and-Half Marabou Minnow	Bob Popovics Lefty Kreh Gene Quigley Clouser/Kreh Dino Torino	All-White, All-Yellow Chartreuse/White Blue/White Gold/White Tan/White
Grass Shrimp Sand Shrimp	½–3" Bait	Ultra Shrimp Clouser Minnow Disco Shrimp	Bob Popovics Bob Clouser Blane Chocolate	Tan/White, All-White, Pink/White Chartreuse/White
Mullet	3–6" (Finger) 7–10" (Cobb) Round Profile Greenish Blue Back Pearl Belly	Siliclone Bucktail Deceiver Bob's Banger	Bob Popovics Bob Popovics Bob Popovics	All-White, Yellow Red Head/White Body Black
Squid	5–12" Bait Translucent Body Large Round Head Long Tentacles Eye in Back	Bucktail Deceiver Shady Lady Tidewater Squid Skok Electric Squid	Bob Popovics Bob Popovics Brian Dowd Dave Skok	Tan. White, Orange Pink/Red, Tan/Purple

DEEP-WATER FLY FISHING

Deep-water fly fishing from a boat is something that every fly fisher struggles with. For some reason, we find it difficult to believe that we can get a fish to hit a fly at depths of greater than 20 feet. Heck, just getting the fly down 20 feet presents its own challenges, let alone having a fish eat the fly while it's there. Deep-water fly fishing is an extremely productive way of catching fish, but it does depend heavily on the right fly line and conditions.

With today's fly lines, it's impossible *not* to be able to fish a fly deep. In the early years, fly lines were only made for floating applications, limiting anglers to the top portion of the water column. The introduction of intermediate lines allowed anglers to peer a bit deeper into the water column with success. Sinking fly lines during the early years were really nothing more than leadcore lines used on the Great Lakes for deep-water salmon and steelhead trolling with conventional tackle. Over the years, fly-line manufactures have developed special fly lines with lead (and now tungsten) heads, attached to floating running lines. Today there are any number of sinking fly lines on the market, ranging from 200 to 1,100 grain.

Your success with deep-water fly fishing comes down to choosing the proper fly line and techniques for deep presentations. Nothing less than a 450-grain sinking line will suffice. In fact, 500 grain, 600 grain, and Rio's new T-14 would all be better choices for depths greater than 20 feet. Our setup for deep-water fly fishing consists of a shooting-head system that starts with Rio's thin-diameter 120-foot clear intermediate running line. A long, thin running line allows you to gain further distances during your cast, and it will sink faster by creating less resistance.

The running line is then connected to a 28-foot shooting head made of Rio's new T-14, a level shooting head that sinks at around 9 inches per second (a little faster than the L-13 leadcore line) and costs only $11 for 30 feet. It is also 1/1,000 inch thinner in diameter, which is why it sinks faster than other lines with the same factory sink rates. Having a weight of 14 grains per foot, it allows you to make your own custom shooting heads depending on the rod weight you intend on using. This makes casting the T-14 shooting head very easy because the total grain weight of the line will now match up to the line specific rod weight (see the chart). Most factory-made sinking fly lines range in sizes from 200 to 1,100 grains. A 200-grain line will sink at a rate of 4 to 5 inches per second, and a 1,000-grain line will sink 9 to 10 inches per second. The concern with the heavier factory lines (600 to 1,000 grains) is that they require 12-weight fly rods to be cast, in addition to slowing down the sink rate down tremendously in faster-moving water. The T-14 will sink very fast and can be cast comfortably with a 10-weight fly rod—use the Rio T-14 chart to match the correct head length.

Rio Products T-14 Head Length Guidelines

6-Weight Fly Rod	15 Feet (210 grains)
7-Weight Fly Rod	18 Feet (252 grains)
8-Weight Fly Rod	21 Feet (294 grains)
9-Weight Fly Rod	25 Feet (350 grains)
10-Weight Fly Rod	28 Feet (392 grains)
11-Weight Fly Rod	32 Feet (448 grains)
12-Weight Fly Rod	36 Feet (504 grains)

Leaders for deep-water fly fishing should be short. We prefer a 3- to 4-foot piece of 20-pound fluorocarbon. We use the fluorocarbon not because the fish are line shy, but rather because it sinks faster than regular monofilament. Longer leaders tend to drag the fly down to the presentation depth. A shorter leader will allow the fly to sink with the line.

The key to the game is to reach the depths where the fish are holding. So how deep are we really talking here? Under the right conditions with the T-14 shooting-head system, we're able to catch fish that are holding in 50 feet of water. The depth you attain will depend on the speed of the currents and the amount of line you can cast. If the fish are holding at 40 feet and your presentation is at 30, chances are you won't connect. The most important factor in reaching fish in deep water is to have a lot of line out in the water. The more line in the water, the deeper it will go.

There is a catch, however. Just having a lot of line out is not enough; you also need a drag-free drift. That means a period of time when your line sinks freely, without any interference from currents or boat drag. To get this, you will need to cast your fly in the direction the boat is drifting. If your T-14 sinks at a rate of 9 inches per second, it will take approximately 35 seconds of drag-free sinking for it to hit 30 feet. By casting your line in the direction the boat is drifting, the line will sink freely by going under the boat and extending back into the drift. This is referred to as a 180-degree upcurrent cast. The faster the current, the longer the cast must be, to adjust for the quicker drift. If your drift is slow and the line seems to be getting stuck on the bottom by casting with a 180-degree cast, cast at a 90-degree angle directly in front or in the back of the boat. This will cut half of the free drift out of the equation and allow you to get to your desired depth without catching bottom.

As in all fly fishing, the right conditions will make all the difference in the world. No matter how hard you try to get a fly line down to these depths, at times high winds and strong currents will prevent you from hitting the target zone. If this happens, one way to minimize drift speed is with a large drift sock or sea anchor. This inexpensive tool can make a tremendous difference when winds or currents become too swift.

WIND AND LINE CONTROL

While deep-water fly fishing can be a challenge to boat anglers, wind presents constant problems for beach and jetty anglers. Because boats are mobile and can generally be positioned upwind or "with" the direction of the cast, boat fly fishers don't seem to struggle with winds and casting as much as their shorebound counterparts.

Whether they're casting from a beach or a jetty, perhaps the biggest mistake anglers make is overcasting into the wind. Casting too hard often results in wide, open loop, which in turn causes slack. The caster cannot catch up, and so is left with little or no retrieve—and possibly a lost fly line around jetties. First, recognize that you will never to be able to cast as far into a headwind as you would on a wind-free day. At the same time, understand that tight loops will get the best results. Take it easy and use only the amount of line you can handle. Find the tempo of the wind and cast when it temporarily subsides for best results. Since it's critical to know where the fly line is at all times, we use lines that are easier to see in the air or on the water. Aim low into the wind so the fly line is closer to the water when it unfolds. This allows it to fall directly where you cast, and it's less likely to be blown back in your direction.

> ### Tip
> When casting a fly in a strong side wind, never position yourself with the wind coming across your casting arm. Turn your body 180 degrees and cast just as you normally would, only make your final cast off your back hand. Keep your arm and wrist straight and accelerate to a quick stop on the final backhaul.

Once the cast is made, line control is critical to your hookup. Anglers who fly fish the open surf know the importance of keeping a tight line throughout the entire retrieve. This especially comes into play when waves are present. Waves and currents have a tendency to push your line back toward the beach, creating large amounts of slack. Just as we find the tempo to the wind, we also try to find a tempo to the surf. Swells and waves always come in sets—most often between three and six waves, depending on the strength of the swell at sea. Make your cast after the last wave in the set. This allows all the white-water to settle and gives you a clean retrieve all the way in to the shore. In addition, turbulence from passing sets will fluster bait that happens to be close to shore. This presents an ambush point for stripers and bluefish.

Line control in fly fishing is best accomplished with a hand-over-hand retrieve. This allows you to keep one hand on the line at all times, never allowing a point of "empty line" during the retrieve. Unlike a single-handed retrieve, the hand-over-hand allows you to control the line at any speed or tempo necessary. You can hold tight and strip very slow, almost crawling the fly or keeping it sweeping with the current; move the fly rapidly at a steady pace; or give the fly a stop-and-start darting action.

Stripping Baskets

Another factor in effective fly-line management is the right stripping basket. Your main concern is to manage and keep track of loose fly line to avoid tangles.

Different stripping baskets are appropriate for different fishing locations. When wading on the flats, where you can be about waist deep in the water, *don't* use baskets with drainholes in the bottom, which allow water to enter; your line will begin to float out. As a result, tangles and knots will develop and your line will be difficult to manage. Choose a hole-free basket instead.

On the jetty and in the surf, on the other hand, the proper stripping basket should have a series of holes in the bottom to aid in quick drainage. This way if water enters into the basket from a breaking wave, it will flow quickly out and not create a safety issue by throwing you off balance. If you construct your own striping basket or modify a manufactured model, make sure not to drill drainholes so large that the fly line falls through.

> ### Tip
> When fishing the surf or the jetty, always use a deep stripping basket with quarter-sized holes drilled in the bottom. This will allow any water from oncoming waves to drain out of the basket quickly, eliminating any resistance while the line is coming out of the basket during the cast.

Your basket should also have some type of cone inserts in the bottom to help keep your fly line separated and tangle-free. This can add distance to your cast, because your line shoots out of the basket unimpeded. The inserts will also help hold your line in place as you move around.

Constructing your own stripping basket is simple. Purchase a small plastic bin 6 to 7 inches deep and approximately 12 by 14 inches in dimension. Get some heavy mono line or weed–cutting line, and drill two holes (3 inches apart) in the bottom of the basket equal to the diameter of the line. Cut 8 to 9 inches of heavy mono and insert them into the two holes; secure with hot glue. Repeat until about five line separators are installed. This will allow line to collect and be cast with greater ease. Then cut two holes for a bungee cord that can be fitted around your waist. You are ready to go.

For those of you who are peering in, waiting for the moment to try salt-water fly fishing, there is no better time than now. Don't be fooled by claims that the sport is too difficult or expensive. Many of our clients who try it for the first time catch fish right off the bat and never look back. Our greatest memories of fly fishing will always be the first years, the time when it is all new and you take everything in like a sponge. You will never forget your first fish on the fly.

18

Planning
Your Trip

We are firm believers that fishing success comes to anglers who are well prepared. When the big bass are blitzing, you don't want to head out with old rusty gear that still has the line on it from last season. Nor would you want to be fishing out in a small boat when a storm is approaching. It's time to discuss the planning or preparation for a successful outing.

Most of us don't fish as often as we'd like. Work, school, and other obligations have a tendency to take us away from our passion for fishing. Being prepared for your outing is thus critical to your success. Start way before the trip to ensure a successful and enjoyable day.

SUCCESSFUL STRATEGIES

The first order of business is getting your gear ready for the season. Hopefully, you have at least rinsed off all the salt from last year; if not, give your rods and reels a good soaking in a warm, lightly soapy tub of fresh water.

Once your gear is cleaned, it's time to inspect your outfits. On the rods, pay particularly close attention to any corrosion that may be forming around the guides. These can become trouble spots down the road if they aren't treated or rewrapped and epoxied. Reels should be stripped down and cleaned with a light oil or reel lubricant. If you're dealing with spinning and conventional outfits, be sure to strip off all the line and put on a fresh batch. As guides, we are on the water close to 200 days a year; we change monofilament on a monthly basis to

Proper preparation before the trip will bring success on the water. Authors
Quigley and Freda show how it's done. Quigley

ensure it does not get dried out and brittle. Nothing is worse that
having the fish of a lifetime on—only to lose it due to faulty tackle.

In addition to the obvious tackle cleaning, there are many other
ways to prepare for the season. Do your plugs have old and rusty treble
hooks on them? Are your waders full of holes and leaks that need
patching? Is your gadget bag ready to go with flashlights, leader material, pliers, nippers, bug spray, and extra terminal tackle?

Boat anglers have a bit more to consider, what with a ship to keep
in tip-top shape in addition to their tackle and accessories. Boat anglers
should be sure to have all of the proper safety equipment on board as
well as a good selection of tackle.

Trip preparation is much different from seasonal preparation. You
don't want to wait all week to go fishing, then finally show up at the dock—
only to find out that winds are blowing out of the northeast 25 to 30 knots
and seas are 6 to 10 feet. Although not all of us are fortunate enough to be
able to pick any day of the week to fish, we can usually narrow it down by
selecting the best day available to us. There are many marine forecast Web
sites today that give anglers both long-range and up-to-the-minute weather
and sea reports; check these prior to planning your trip.

Tides and moon phases also play an important role in a successful
outing. Showing up at the beach for a quick two-hour fishing session at

dead low tide probably isn't the best choice for most anglers. Likewise, you probably wouldn't want to fish the high tide on full moon in spring—water levels can fluctuate upward of 8 feet on either side of the tide at that time of year.

> **Tip**
> Turn down the drags on all your reels at the end of every season. This will take the tension off the components and prolong the life of your reels for many seasons to come. Should your fly reels have cork drags, store them in a warm area and always keep the cork moist with the manufacturer's recommended lubricant or oil.

So what does all this mean when it comes to planning your fishing trip? Use common sense and the tools that have been given to you through marine weather forecasts and Internet sites, and be sure that your gear is in the best working order it can be.

SO WHY HIRE A GUIDE?

There are many reasons to hire a guide. Whether it be simply going out and catching fish, learning how to fly fish or improve your cast, or discovering a new hot spot or technique of fishing, guides offer anglers many different avenues to enjoy fishing.

Many anglers think that fishing guides have the life. True, it's a very rewarding profession, but have no doubts about it: It's also a tough and rigorous job that offers a whole other world of pressures. A guide's day starts and ends way before you show up at the dock or on the beach. On a typical charter, we arrive at our boats at least an hour and a half before the charter starts in order to fuel up, rig outfits, network with other captains, and ensure that all our gear and safety equipment is in perfect working order.

Probably the single most important factor that makes a good guide is knowledge. Most guides, if they are worth their weight, have spent their entire lives fishing a particular area or technique and know it exhaustively. Good guides know their waters better than anyone else. They know where the fish bite when the wind blows south. They know where the fish bite when the tide is high or low. They know what turns the bite on, and what turns the bite off. Good guides know their tackle, knots, rigging, and boat like no other. Guides spend a good portion of their downtime on the water scouting and observing patterns when they're not with paying customers, all to ensure a productive day on the water when it's game day.

> **Tip**
> When hiring a guide for the day, always find out ahead of time who is responsible for bringing lunch and beverages. Many guides in the Southeast require that the clients bring lunch, while guides in the Northeast supply lunch and soft drinks for full-day charters.

More and more people are getting into saltwater fishing every day, and the days of captains standing behind the wheel and barking at a customer for dropping a fish or losing a lure are long over. You're paying your guide to go out and have a good time, and it's our job to ensure that you do so—with or without fish in the box at the end of the day. A good guide can read clients' angling ability quickly, and offer fishing situations that are not over their heads. If anglers are having trouble casting, or are making mistakes with the equipment, it's a guide's job to show them the right way. A good guide coaches with confidence rather than criticism. Nothing is worse than a cocky guide with an *I-am-the-greatest-fisherman-of-all-time* attitude. If clients don't overcome a challenge or learn the proper techniques on our trips, it's *our* fault—we didn't do our job as teachers.

> **Tip**
> Never step onto a guide's boat with black-soled shoes or black-soled sneakers. These shoe bottoms leave marks on nonskid decks that take hours of hard work to remove.

When it comes time to choose a guide, spend some time researching the right one. Don't be afraid to call guides on the phone or shoot off an e-mail asking questions about the type of fishing they do, the kind of tackle they use, and the methods with which they set out to catch fish. If you are looking for personable one-on-one instruction while you fish, it would probably not be a good choice to book a party boat for the day. These crews are extremely knowledgeable, but they're generally dealing with up to 60 clients while still managing to navigate a 70-foot boat. Instead, a guide who takes one to three anglers on a smaller boat would be a better choice. Likewise, if you're looking to bait fish or troll wire line for stripers in fall, a fly-fishing guide most likely wouldn't suit your needs.

Don't be afraid to hire a guide in your local area to find out where to go. If that's your intention, mention it to the guide up front so he knows you're looking to fish a multitude of spots, and hear about when they generally fish well. It's also important to tell your guide up front what your fishing ability is. Be as honest as you can here. Guides don't care either way whether you're a beginner or an expert. They will take you fishing regardless, but they do need to know your ability so they can put you in appropriate situations.

In the New Jersey, New York, and Connecticut coastal areas, a group of guides has formed the Professional Fly and Light Tackle Guides Association (PFLGA). The PFLGA (www.light-tacklemagazine.com) comprises the best fly- and light-tackle-fishing guides in the tristate area. These guides and captains have earned their stripes and rank as

Flyrodder Pete DeStefano casts into the striper rich New Jersey surf. Quigley

some of the best in the country. Currently more than 45 guides have been accepted into this prestigious organization. Not just any guide can join the PFLGA; guides must apply, then go through a peer screening in order to qualify. We urge anyone who is interested in getting a guide in the future to hire a PFLGA-certified guide. By doing so, you are assured a professional captain or guide who can offer you a safe, productive, and enjoyable day on the water.

ABOUT THE AUTHORS

CAPTAIN JIM FREDA

Jim is a U.S.C.G. licensed Captain. He has been fishing the inshore waters of the Jersey Shore for over 25 years. Jim is on the national Pro Staff for St. Croix Rod Company, Spotters Sunglasses, Aussie Tackle, AVET Conventional Reels, and Korkers. Jim is a noted author, highly sought-after seminar speaker, fishing columnist, and outdoor writer. His first book, *Fishing the New Jersey Coast* is a best seller on the market today. Jim contributes regularly to *Fly Fishing in Saltwaters Magazine*, *Fly Fisherman* Magazine, and *The Fisherman* Magazine. He has also written for *NJ Angler* Magazine and *NJ Boating and Fishing* Magazine. His saltwater fishing columns appear in The Bergen Record, Asbury Park Press, and Coast Star Newspapers. Jim is a member of the Atlantic Saltwater Flyrodders and Manasquan Fishing Club. He resides in Manasquan with his wife Mary and three children, Christie, Carlie, and Thomas James.

CAPTAIN GENE QUIGLEY

Gene is a U.S.C.G. licensed Captain and is considered one of the top fly and light-tackle guides in the northeast. A native of the Jersey Shore, Captain Gene has been fishing the inshore and offshore waters for over 25 years. A noted author, photographer, and seminar speaker, he contributes regularly to *Fly Fishing in Saltwaters* Magazine, *Fly Fisherman* Magazine, *The Fisherman* Magazine, and is a featured speaker on the Sport Fishing Magazine's "Learn From the Experts" Seminar Series. Gene also has a fishing column in the Asbury Park Press. Captain Gene sits on the national factory team for St. Croix Rod Company, and is on the national pro staff for Parker Boats, Tibor Reels, AVET Conventional Reels, Rio Fly Lines, Spotters Sunglasses, Patagonia, and Korkers. He is currently the Director of the New Jersey Professional Fly & Light Tackle Guides Association and sits on the association's national Board of Directors. He is also a member of the Atlantic Saltwater Flyrodders. Gene resides in Toms River with his wife Cecilia and two children, Justin and Patrick.

SHELL E. CARIS

Shell E. Caris got interested in saltwater fishing in 1953 when he caught his first striped bass from the surf in Belmar, NJ. Shell E. has over 50 years of surf and jetty experience and is on national pro staff for G. Loomis, Korkers, and Spotters Sunglasses. He is a member of the Atlantic Saltwater Flyrodders and past president of the Berkeley Striper Club in NJ. Shell E. is a frequent contributor to *The Fisherman* Magazine and has written numerous arti-cles on surf and jetty strategies. He also owns and operates Dinette World Furniture Store in Bricktown for over 34 years. Shell E. resides in Toms River with his wife Bonnie.